DISCOVERING FLORENCE ITALY

The Cradle of The Renaissance

PICTORIAL SEARIES

Presented by

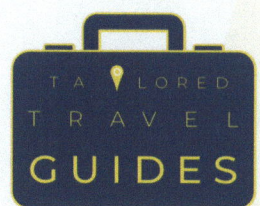

Discover your journey!

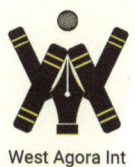

a WEST AGORA INT S.R.L. Brand
www.tailoredtravelguides.com
Edited by WEST AGORA INT S.R.L.
WEST AGORA INT S.R.L. All Rights Reserved
Copyright © WEST AGORA INT S.R.L., 2023

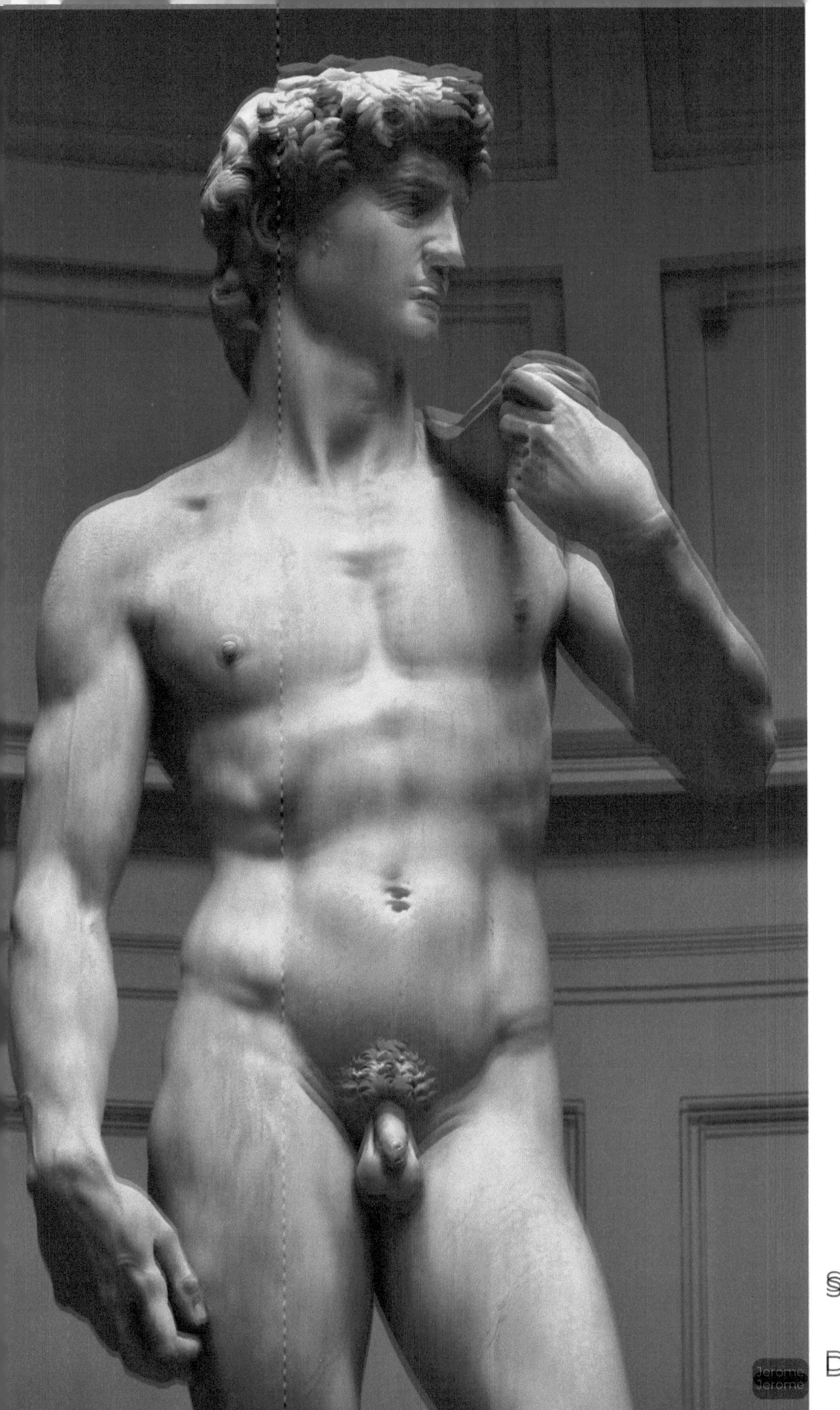

Statue of David
in Galleria
Dell'Accademia

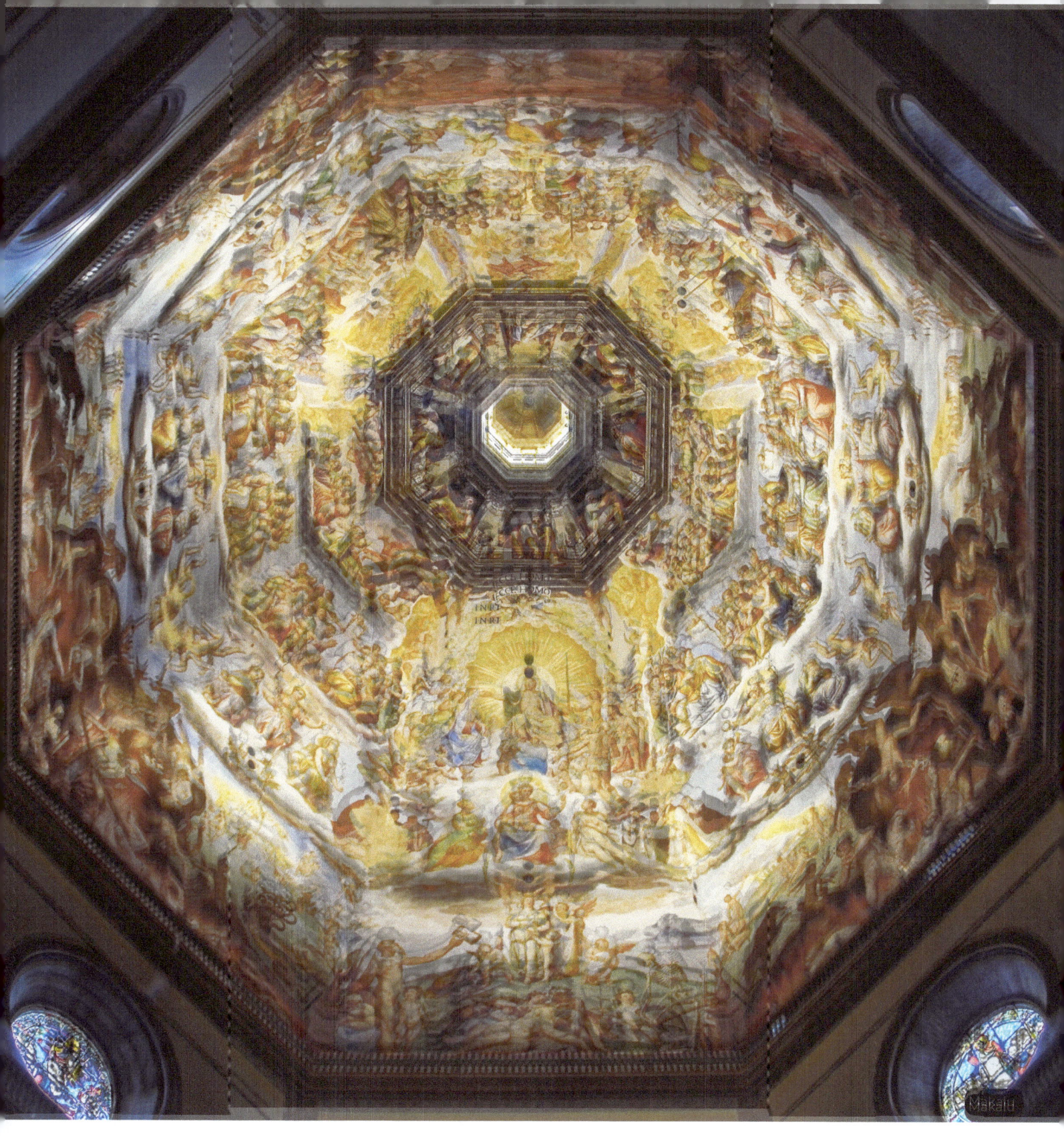

Fresco inside the Santa Maria Novella Cathedral

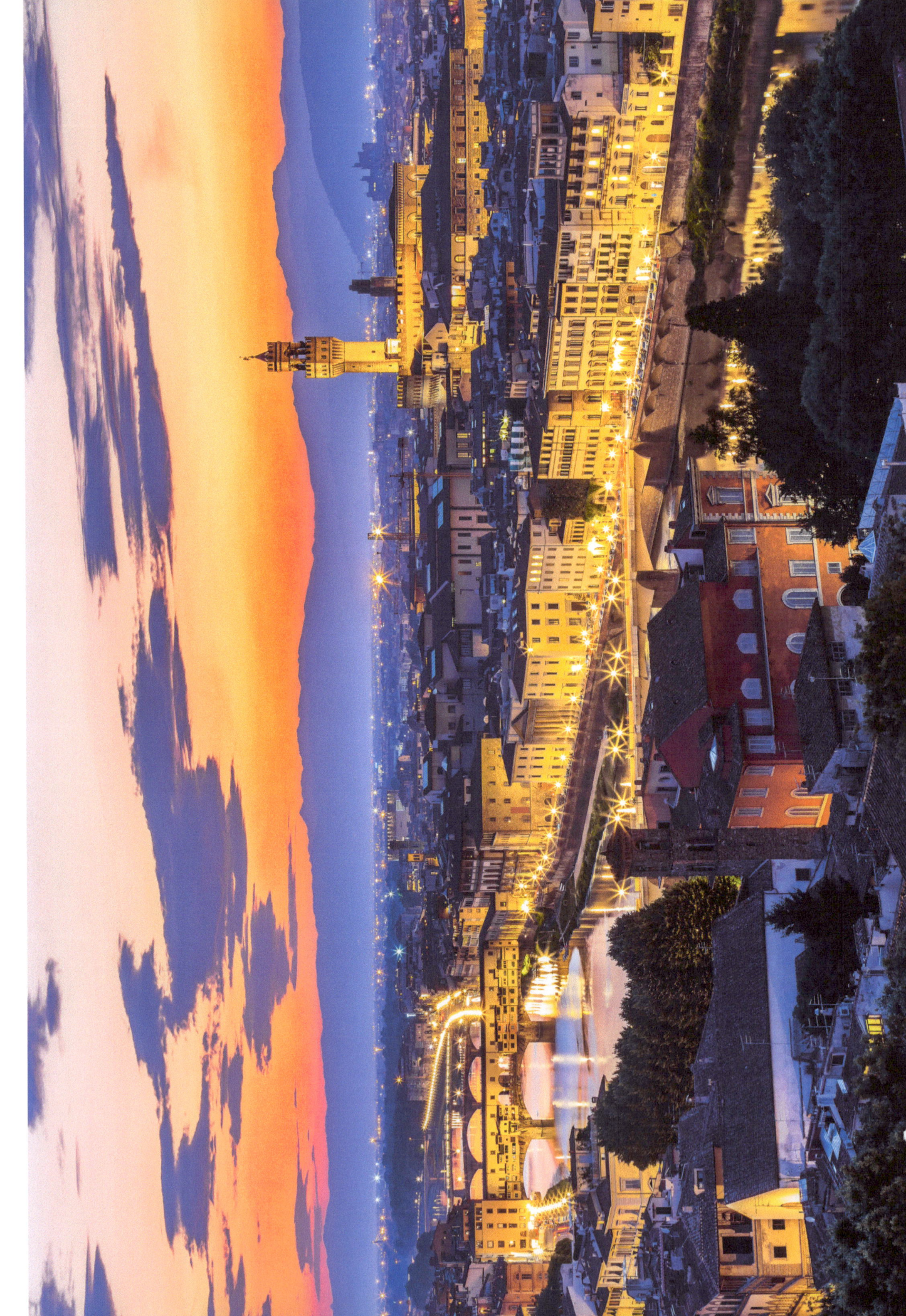

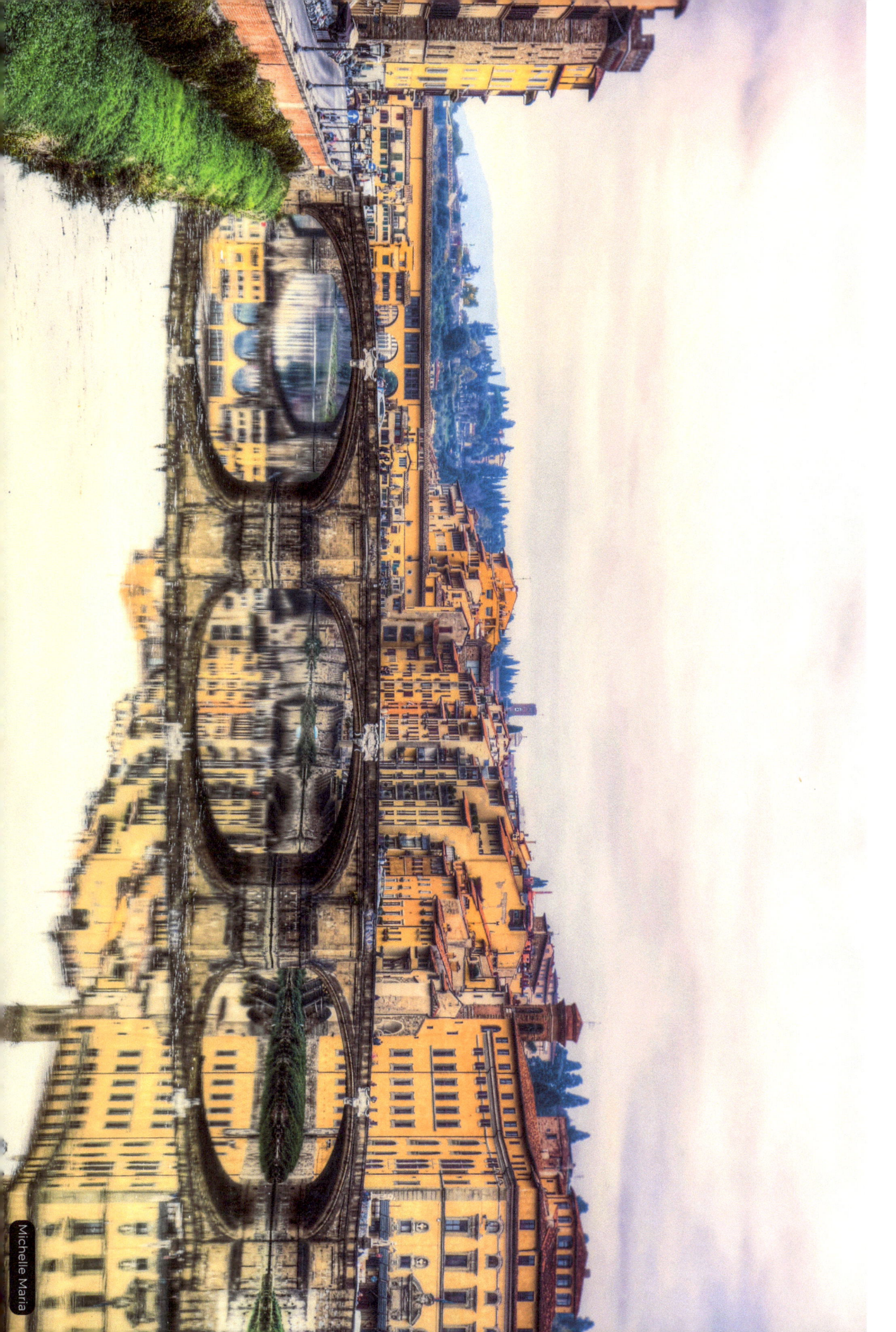

Ponte Vecchio

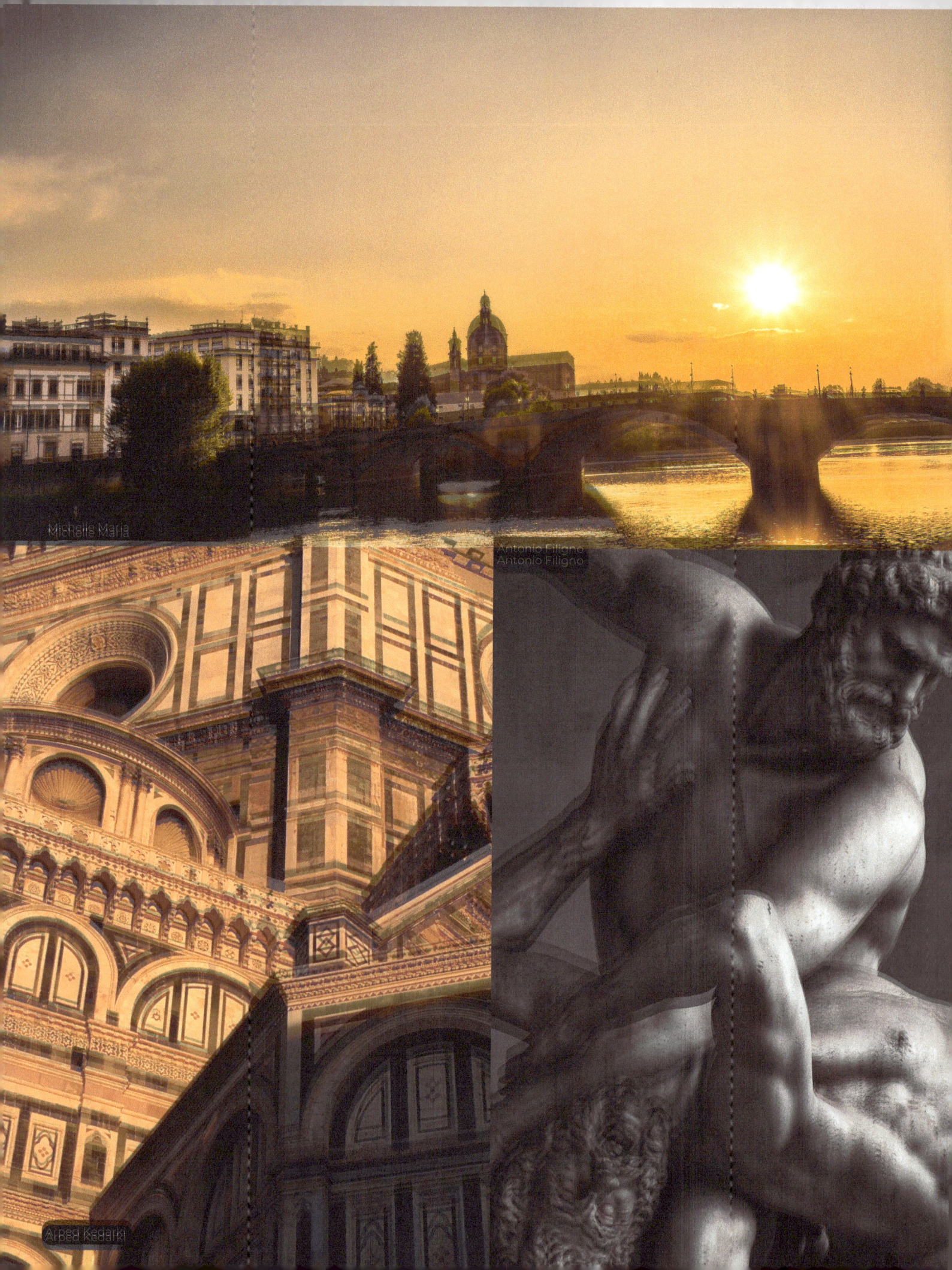

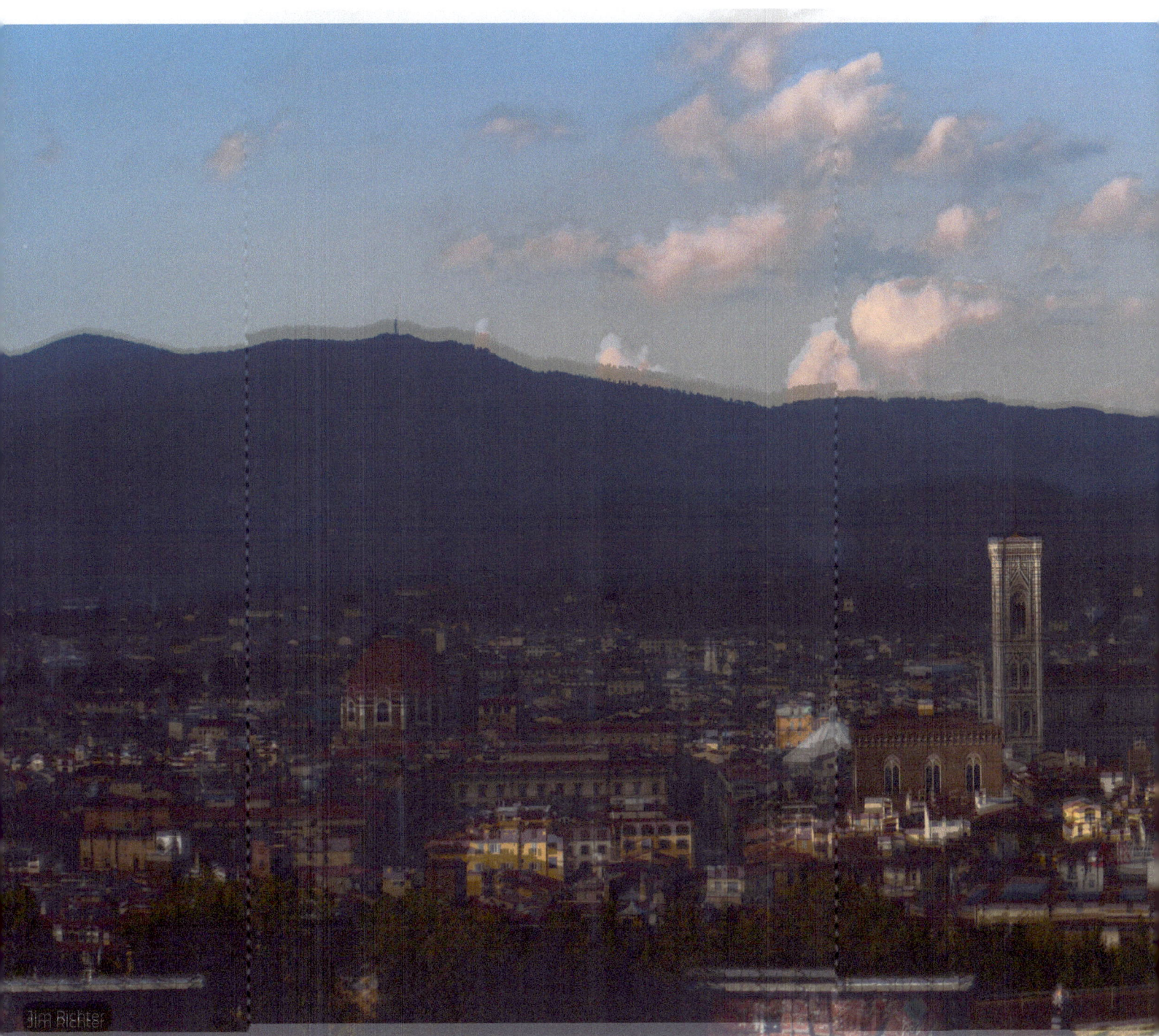

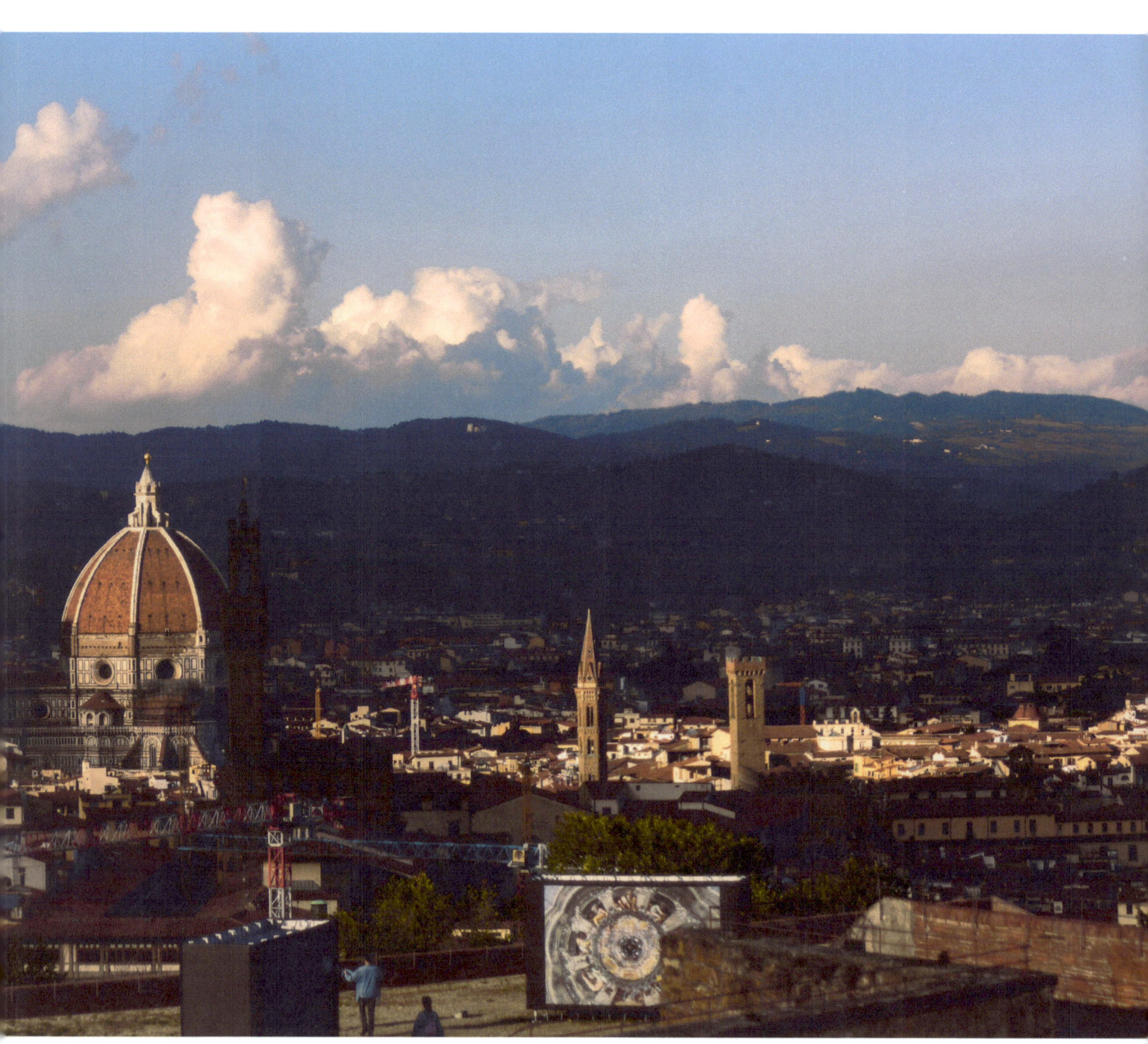

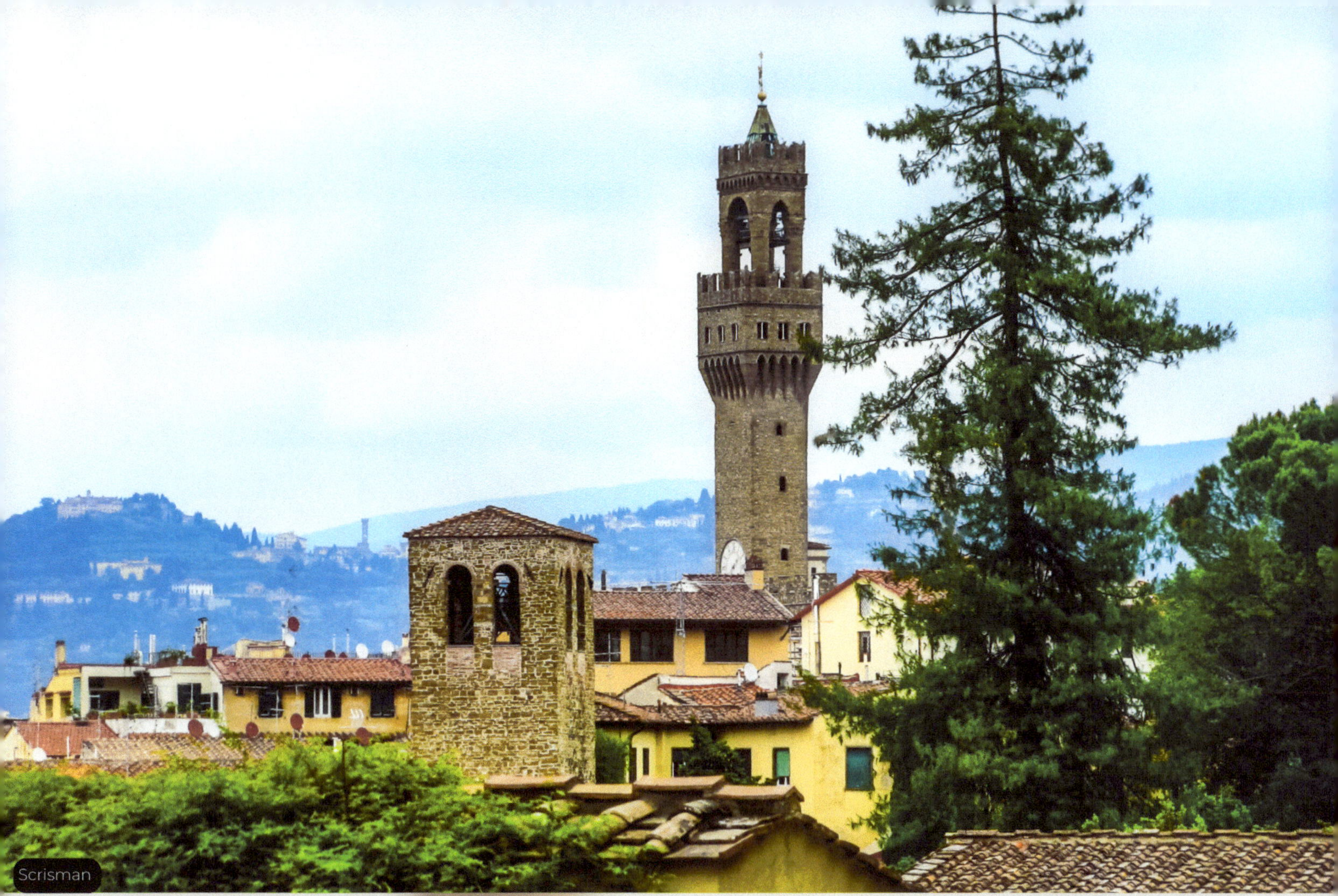

Scrisman

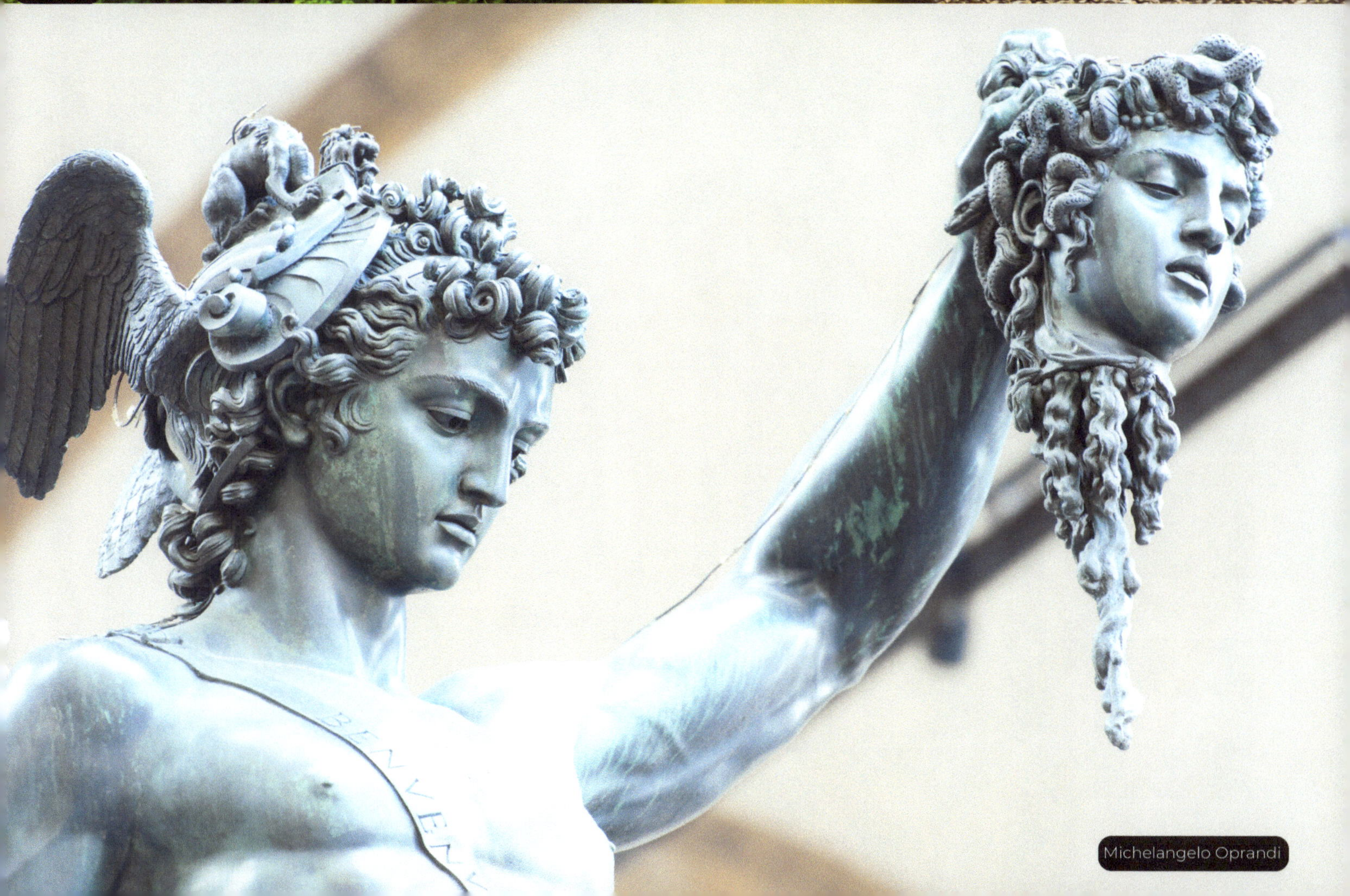

Michelangelo Oprandi

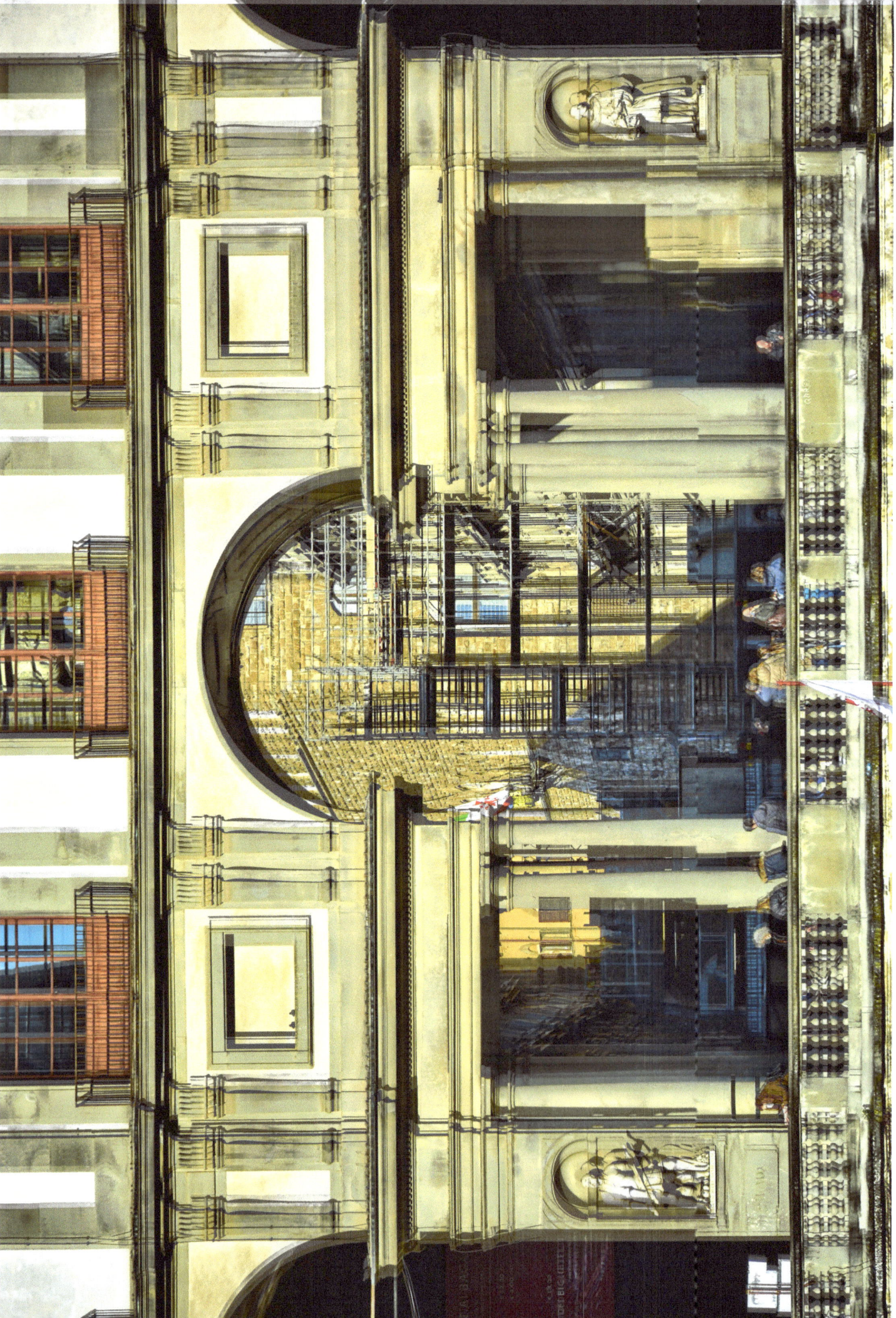

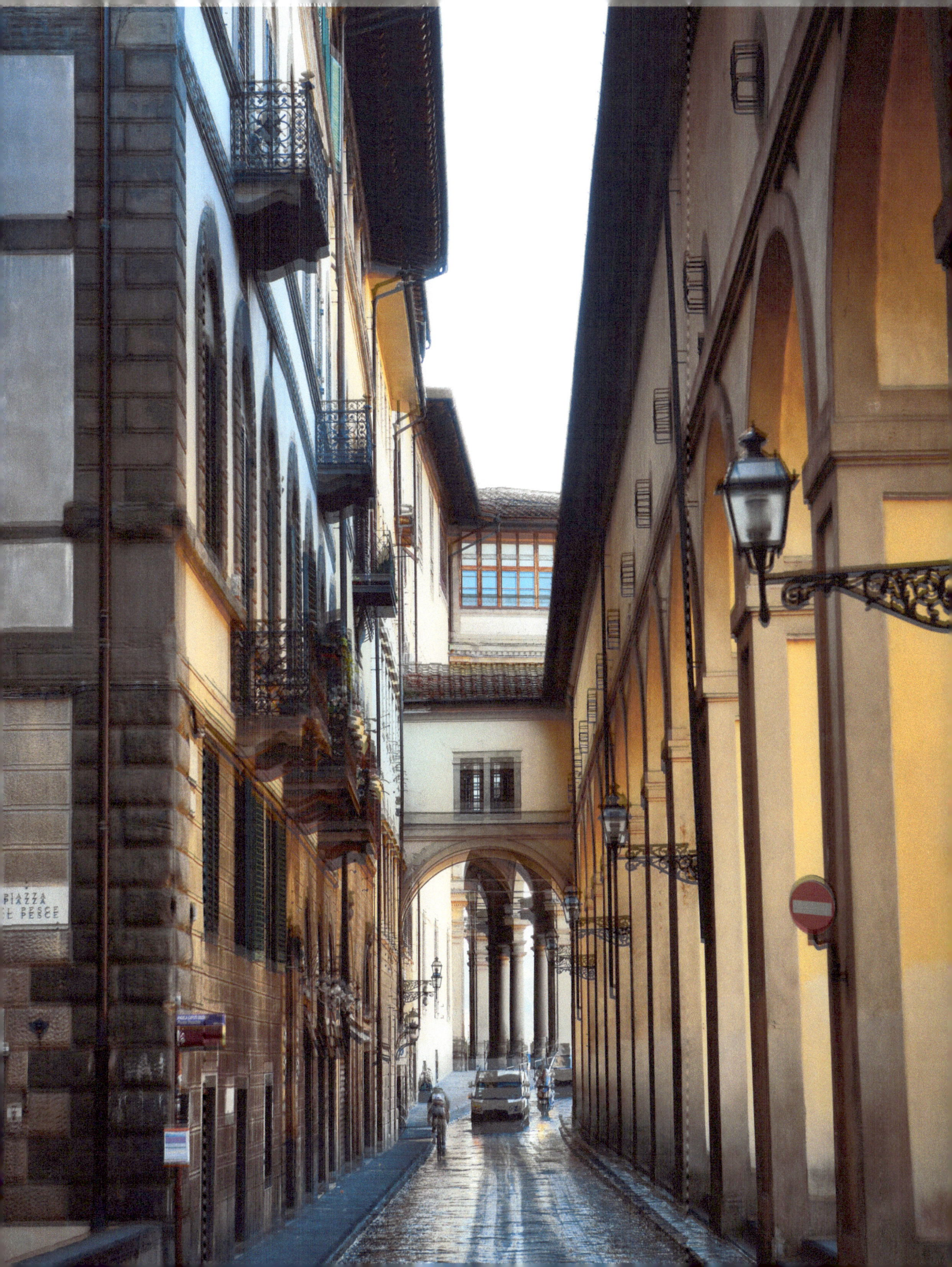

Florence Cathedral

The Florence Cathedral, known as the Cattedrale di Santa Maria del Fiore, stands as a majestic symphony in marble, harmonizing Gothic and Renaissance architectural elements. Its grandeur not only dominates the skyline of Florence but also encapsulates the artistic and cultural zenith of the Renaissance.

Initiated in 1296, designed by Arnolfo di Cambio, and completed in the 15th century, this cathedral is a masterpiece of construction. Its vast scale, complex engineering, and aesthetic beauty represent an unparalleled architectural feat of its time. The exterior, a mesmerizing interplay of white, green, and pink marble, creates an enchanting geometric pattern, a testament to the exquisite craftsmanship and artistic vision of the era.

The cathedral's most striking feature is its monumental dome, engineered by Filippo Brunelleschi. This innovative dome not only crowns the cathedral but also symbolizes the ingenuity of Renaissance thinkers and architects. Inside, the cathedral's vast nave impresses with its sheer size and simplicity, directing all attention upwards to the magnificent dome.

Stepping inside Florence Cathedral is like entering a realm where art, history, and spirituality converge. The intricate stained glass windows, the detailed frescoes, and the serene ambience offer a glimpse into the soul of Florence, a city where art and faith have intertwined for centuries.

Florence Cathedral is more than a religious edifice; it is a beacon of human achievement, a source of inspiration, and a key chapter in the narrative of the Renaissance.

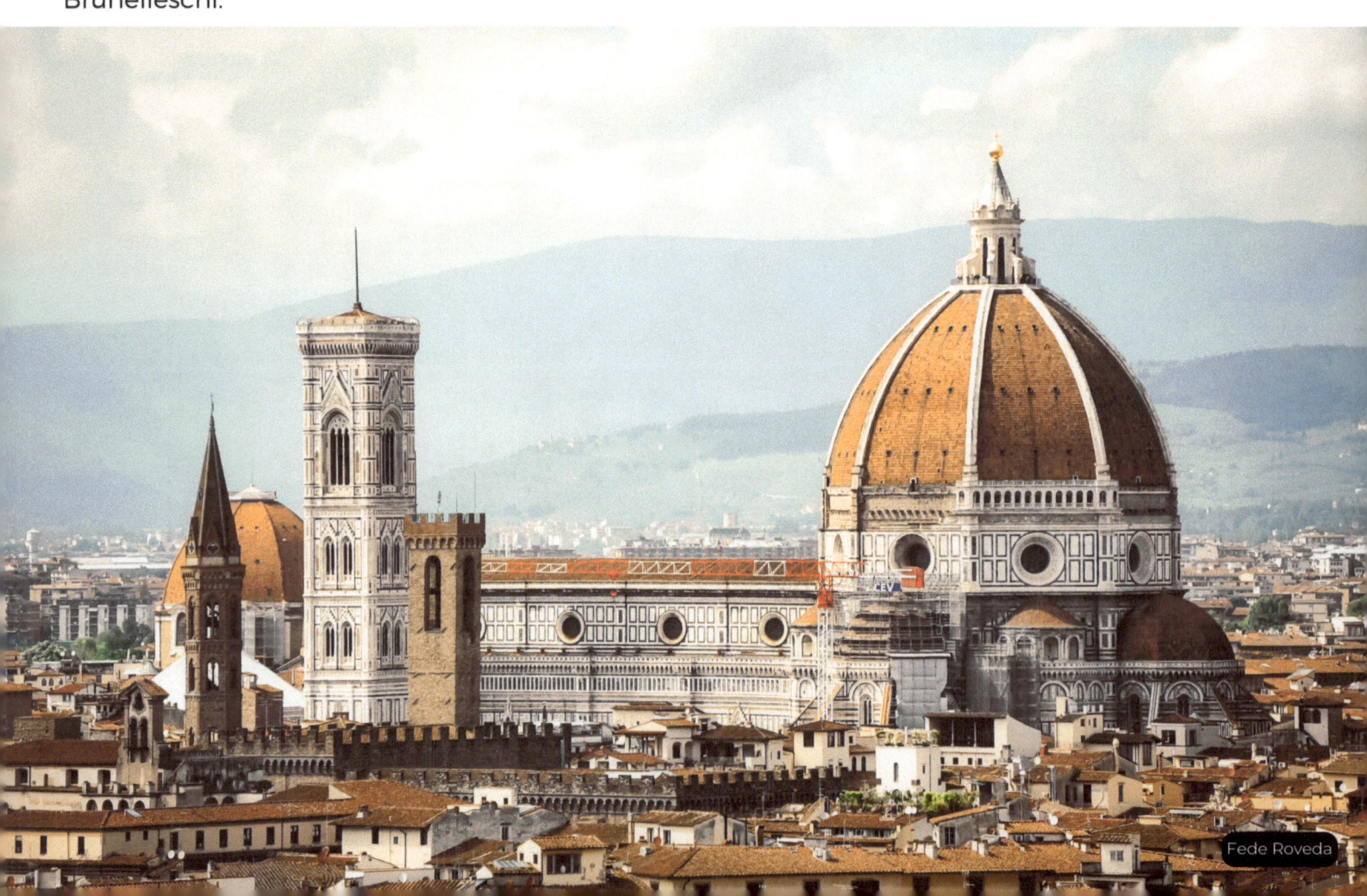

Fede Roveda

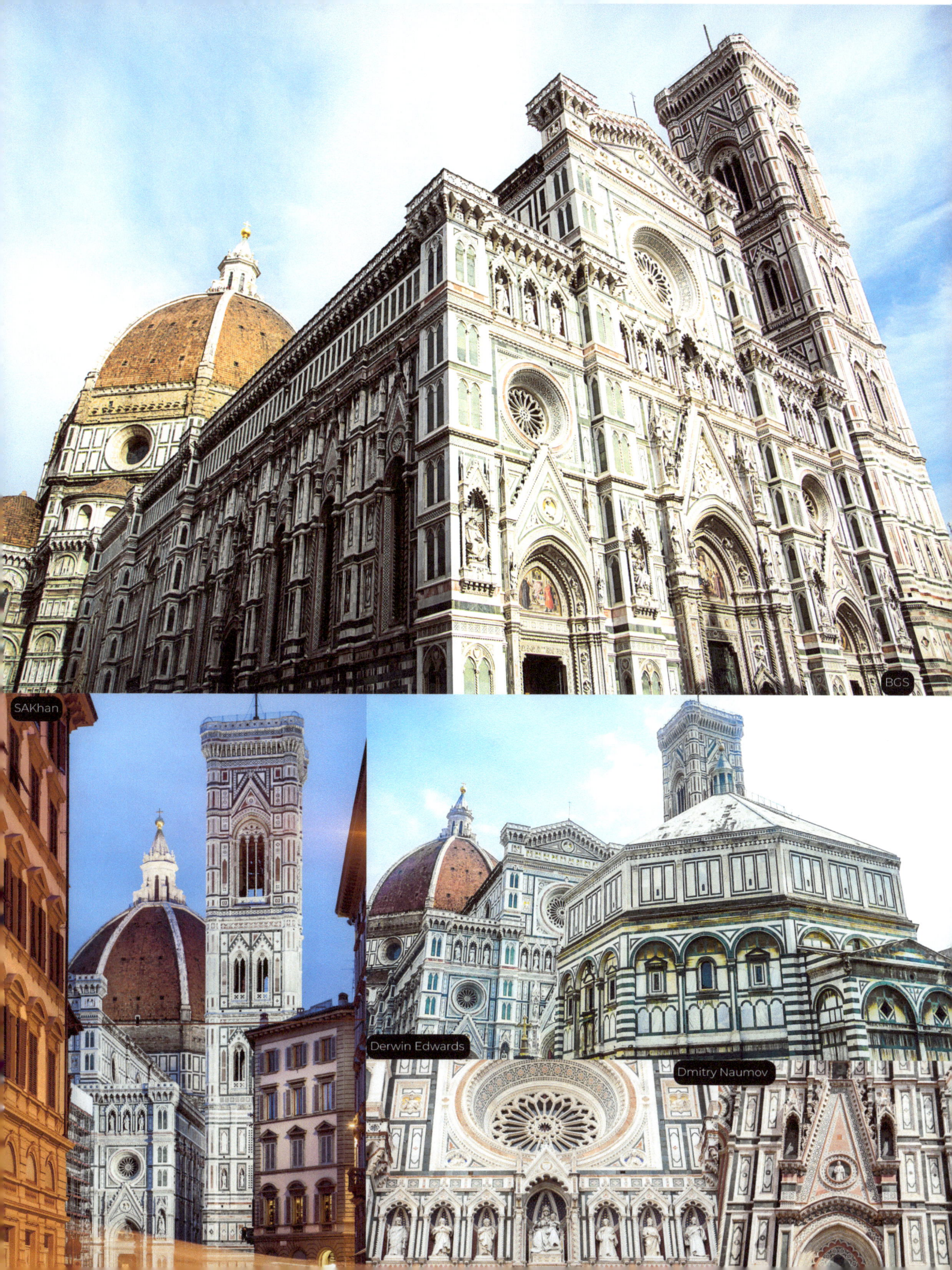

Ponte Vecchio

The Ponte Vecchio, an enduring symbol of Florence, stretches gracefully over the Arno River, a testament to the city's medieval craftsmanship and Renaissance splendor. Dating back to 1345, this bridge is not just a vital passageway but a historical treasure trove, capturing the essence of Florence's storied past. Characterized by its unique design, the bridge is famed for its array of shops, traditionally occupied by goldsmiths and jewelers, a tradition dating back to the Medici era. These quaint shops, with their wooden shutters and overhanging signs, offer a picturesque scene, evoking images of a time when merchants and artisans were the heartbeat of the city.

The Ponte Vecchio's robust stone arches have withstood the test of time, surviving floods and wars, standing as a resilient symbol of Florence's endurance. The bridge's upper level houses the Vasari Corridor, a secret passageway built for the Medici family, linking the Palazzo Vecchio with the Palazzo Pitti.

Strolling across the Ponte Vecchio is like walking through a living museum, surrounded by the rich history and vibrant culture of Florence. The views from the bridge are unparalleled, offering panoramic vistas of the Arno River and the city's historic buildings, a captivating spectacle at sunset.

The Ponte Vecchio is not just a bridge but a timeless icon, encapsulating the artistic spirit and historical depth of Florence, leaving an indelible impression on all who wander its path.

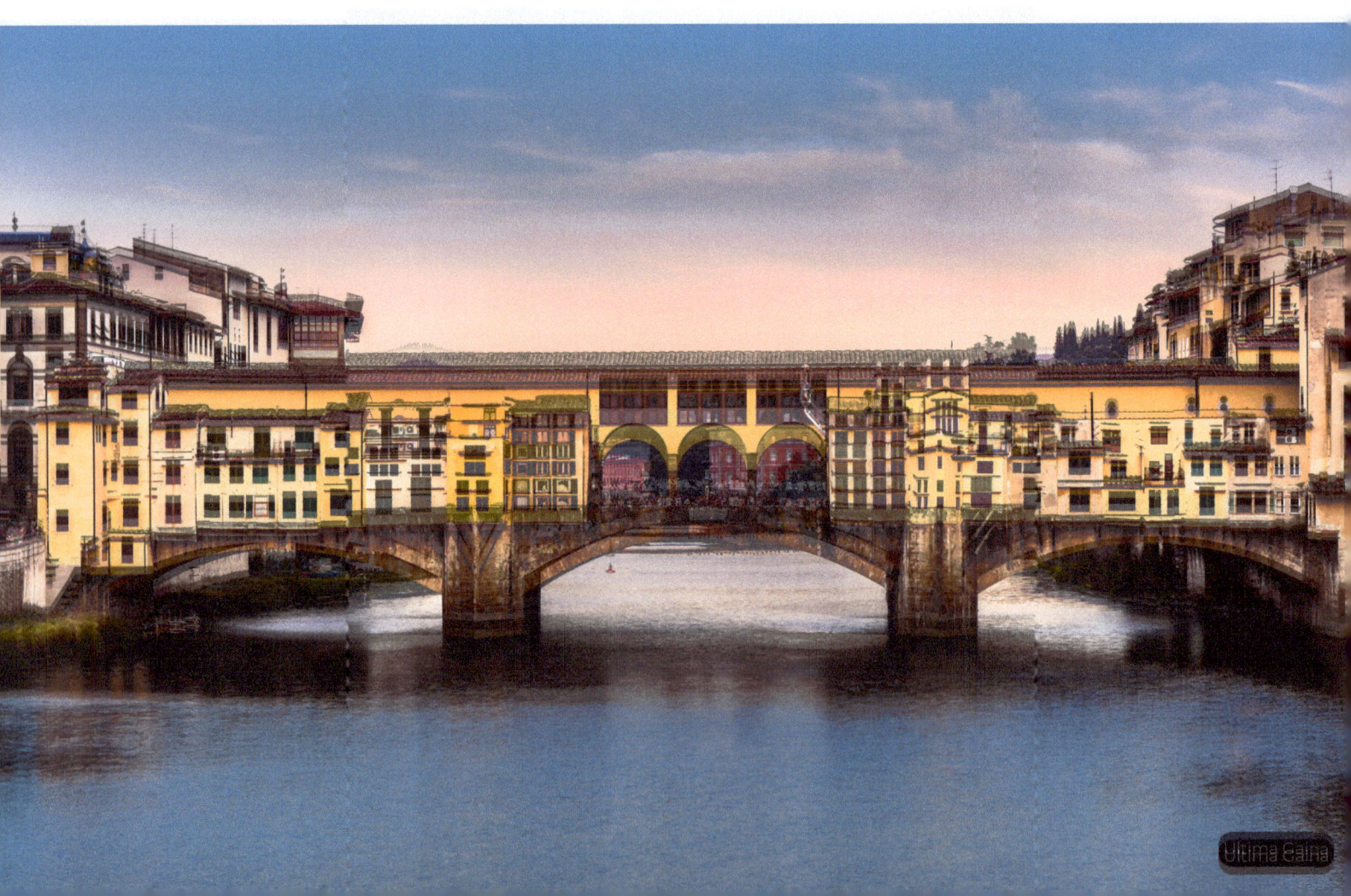

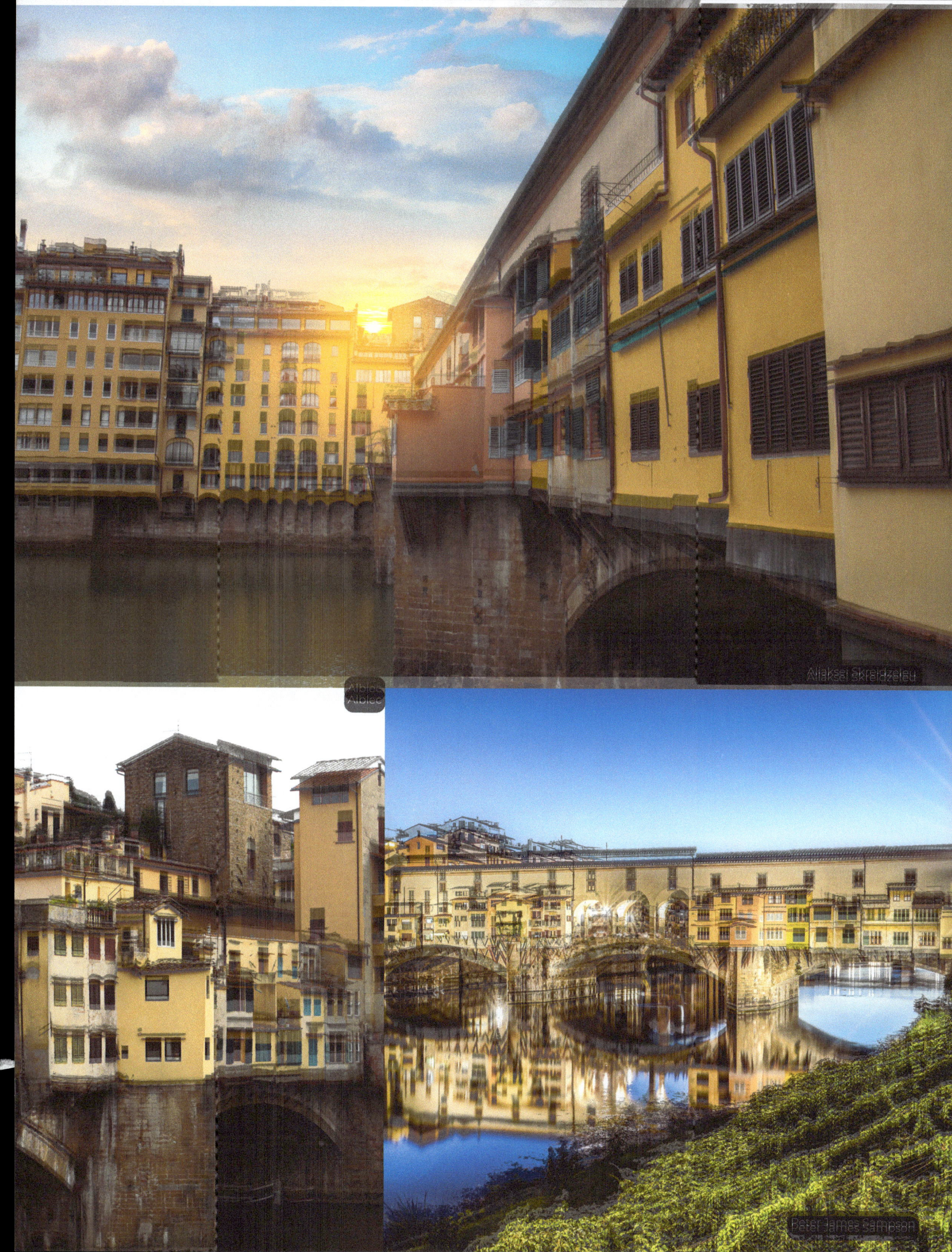

Isolatto in Bobli Gardens Park

Dimitry Naumov

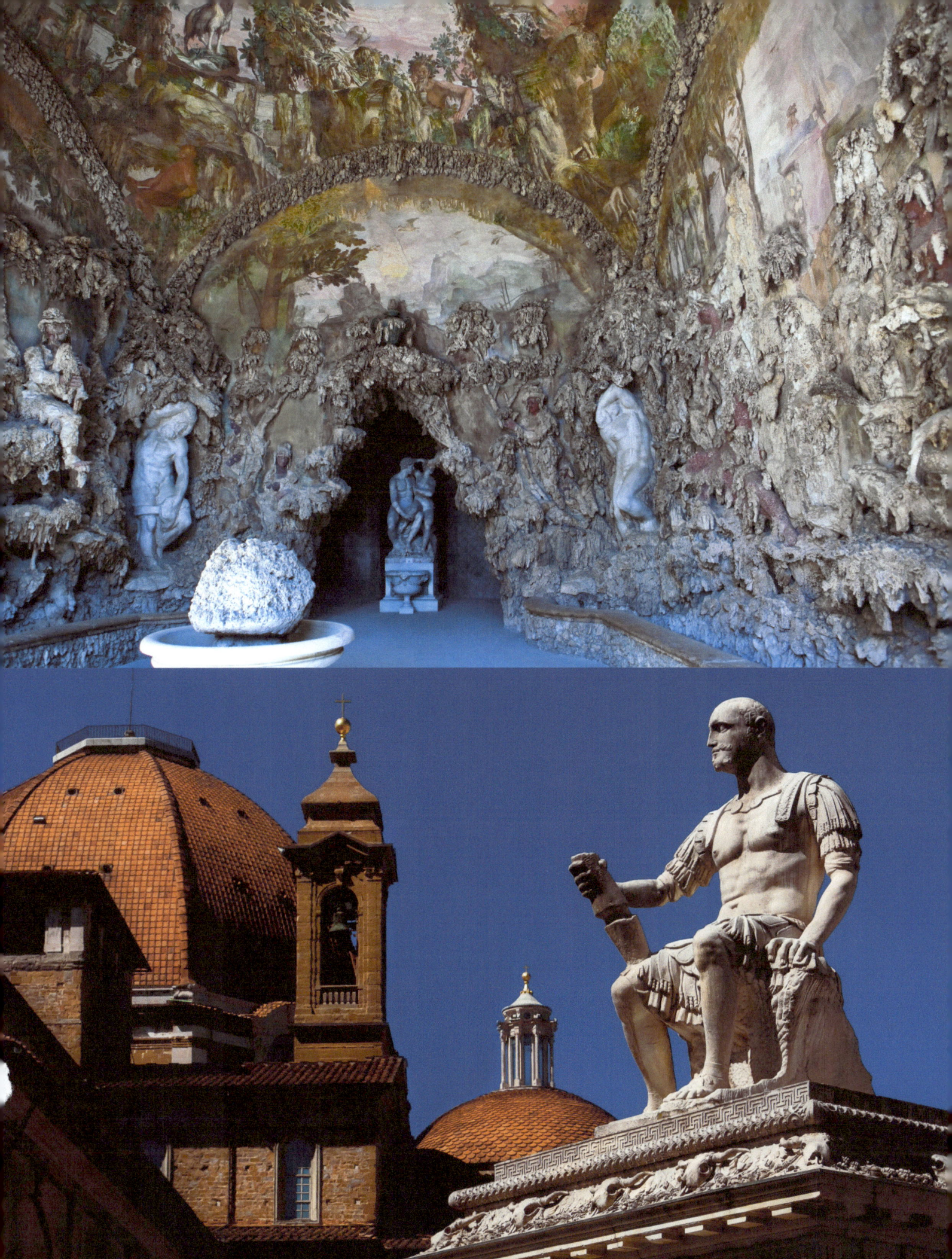

Palazzo Vecchio

In the heart of Florence's Piazza della Signoria stands the Palazzo Vecchio, a monumental testament to the city's rich political history and artistic heritage. Originally built in the early 14th century as the seat of the city's government, this fortress-like palace symbolizes the enduring strength and influence of Florence through the ages.

The Palazzo Vecchio, with its robust crenellated battlements and towering Arnolfo Tower, presents a formidable yet elegant façade. This architectural masterpiece combines elements of medieval fortifications with the refined aesthetics of the Renaissance. The tower, soaring 94 meters high, offers breathtaking views of Florence, a panoramic spectacle of the city's red rooftops and winding streets.

Stepping inside, the Palazzo Vecchio reveals a world of opulent chambers, grand halls, and exquisite art. The elaborately decorated rooms, such as the Salone dei Cinquecento, are adorned with masterpieces by renowned artists like Michelangelo and Vasari, reflecting the artistic brilliance of the Renaissance. Each room tells a story, a narrative of power, artistry, and intrigue that shaped Florence's history.

The Palazzo Vecchio is not merely a historical building; it's a journey through time, where each stone, artwork, and fresco narrates the legacy of Florence's past rulers and their aspirations. This palace stands as a symbol of Florentine pride, a timeless reminder of the city's enduring allure and cultural magnificence.

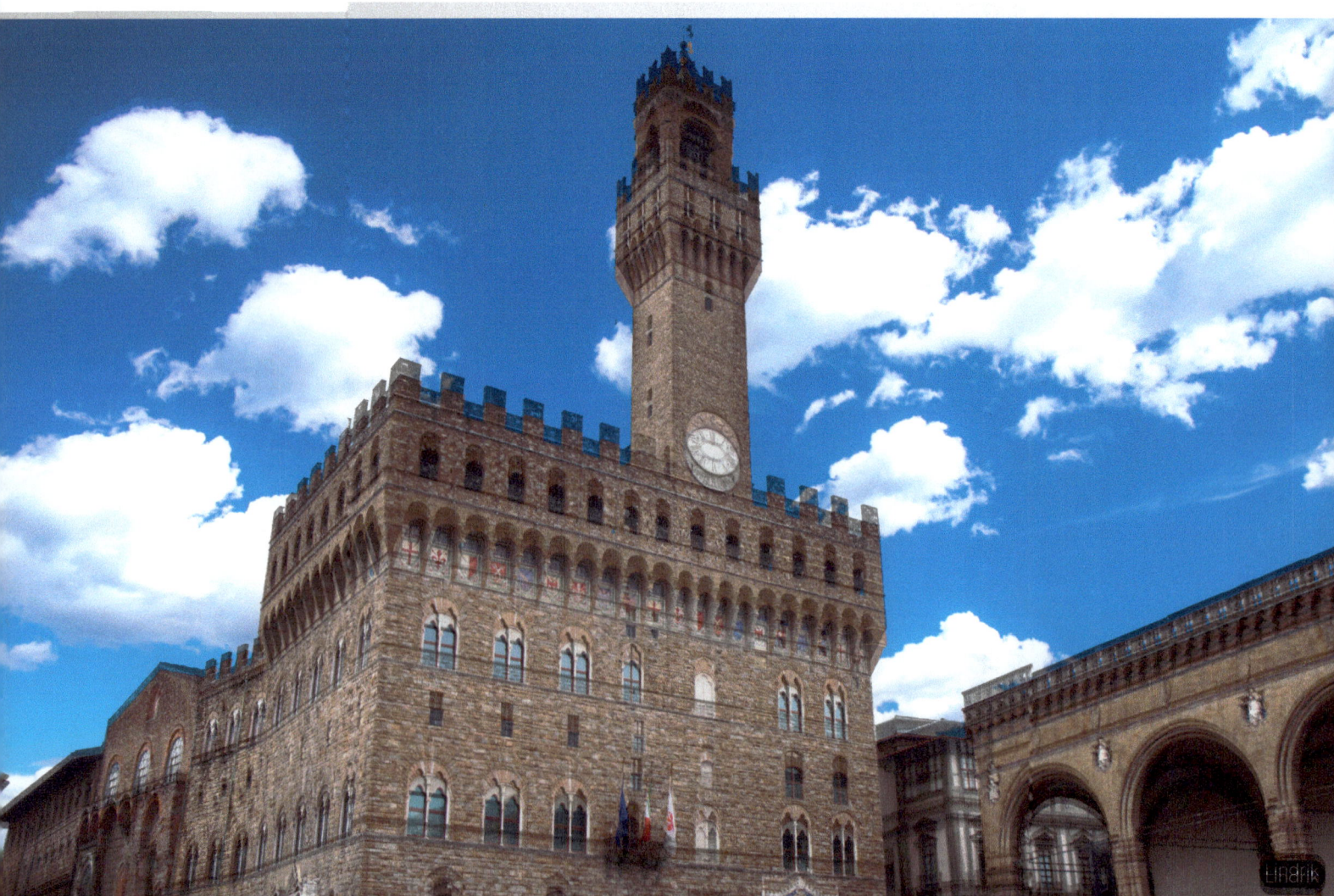

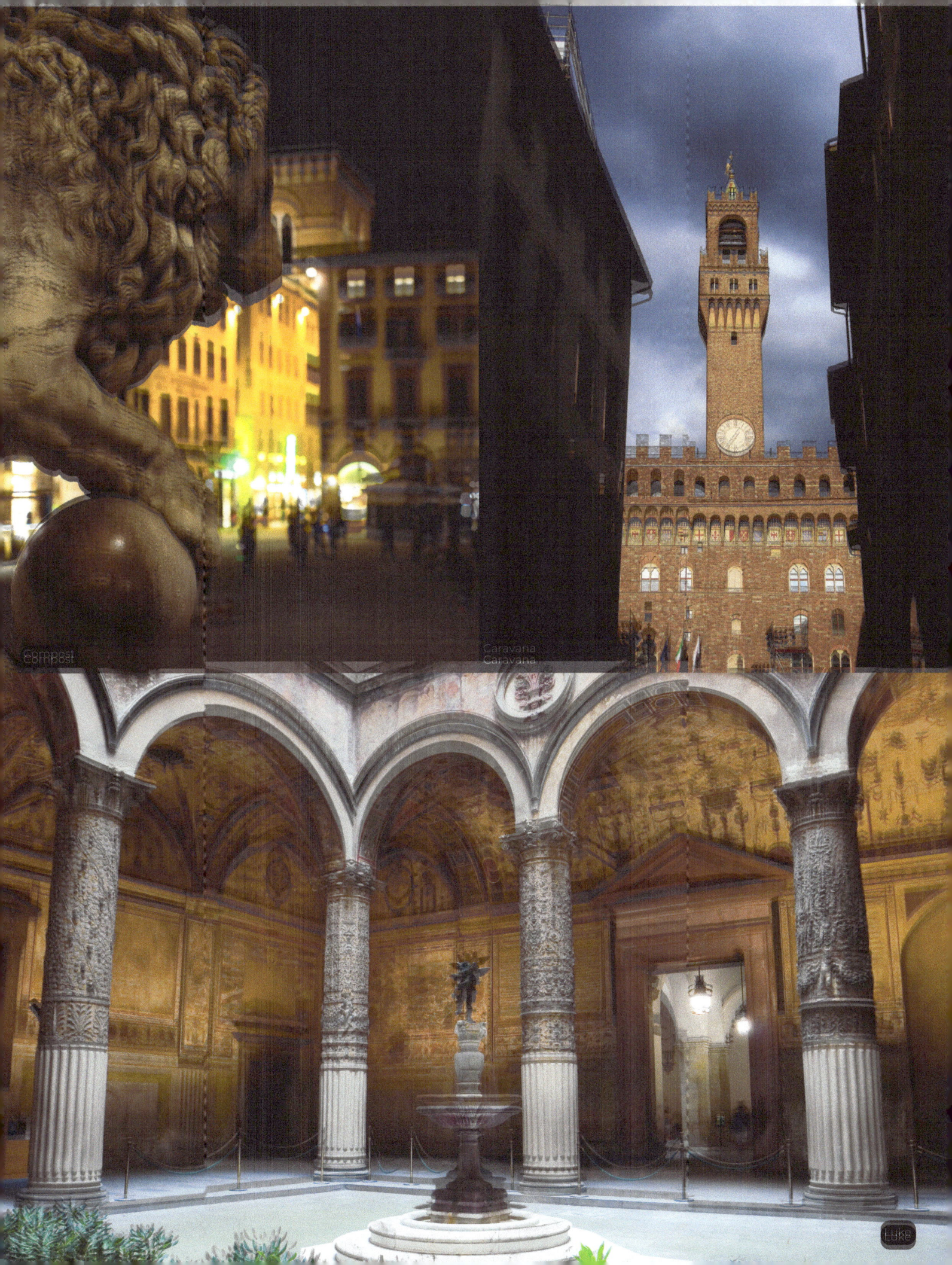

Medici Chapels

Nestled within the Basilica of San Lorenzo, the Medici Chapels stand as an opulent tribute to one of Florence's most influential families, the Medicis. Constructed in the 16th and 17th centuries, these chapels are not just burial places but a fusion of art, architecture, and history, showcasing the grandeur of the Medici legacy.

The New Sacristy, designed by Michelangelo, is an architectural marvel. Here, Michelangelo's sculptural genius is on full display, with masterpieces such as the allegorical statues of Day, Night, Dawn, and Dusk guarding the tombs of Giuliano and Lorenzo de' Medici. The sculptures exude a poignant blend of human emotion and divine beauty, a hallmark of Michelangelo's work.

The Chapel of the Princes, a later addition, is a dazzling display of opulence. Its dome, one of the largest in Florence, is adorned with intricate frescoes. The chapel's interior is a spectacle of richly colored marble, semi-precious stones, and detailed mosaics, reflecting the wealth and power of the Medici dynasty.

Visiting the Medici Chapels is a journey through the heart of the Renaissance, where art and power intertwine. Each chapel tells a part of the Medici story, their patronage of the arts, and their enduring impact on Florence. The chapels are not only a resting place for the Medici family but a testament to their lasting legacy in shaping the cultural and artistic landscape of Florence.

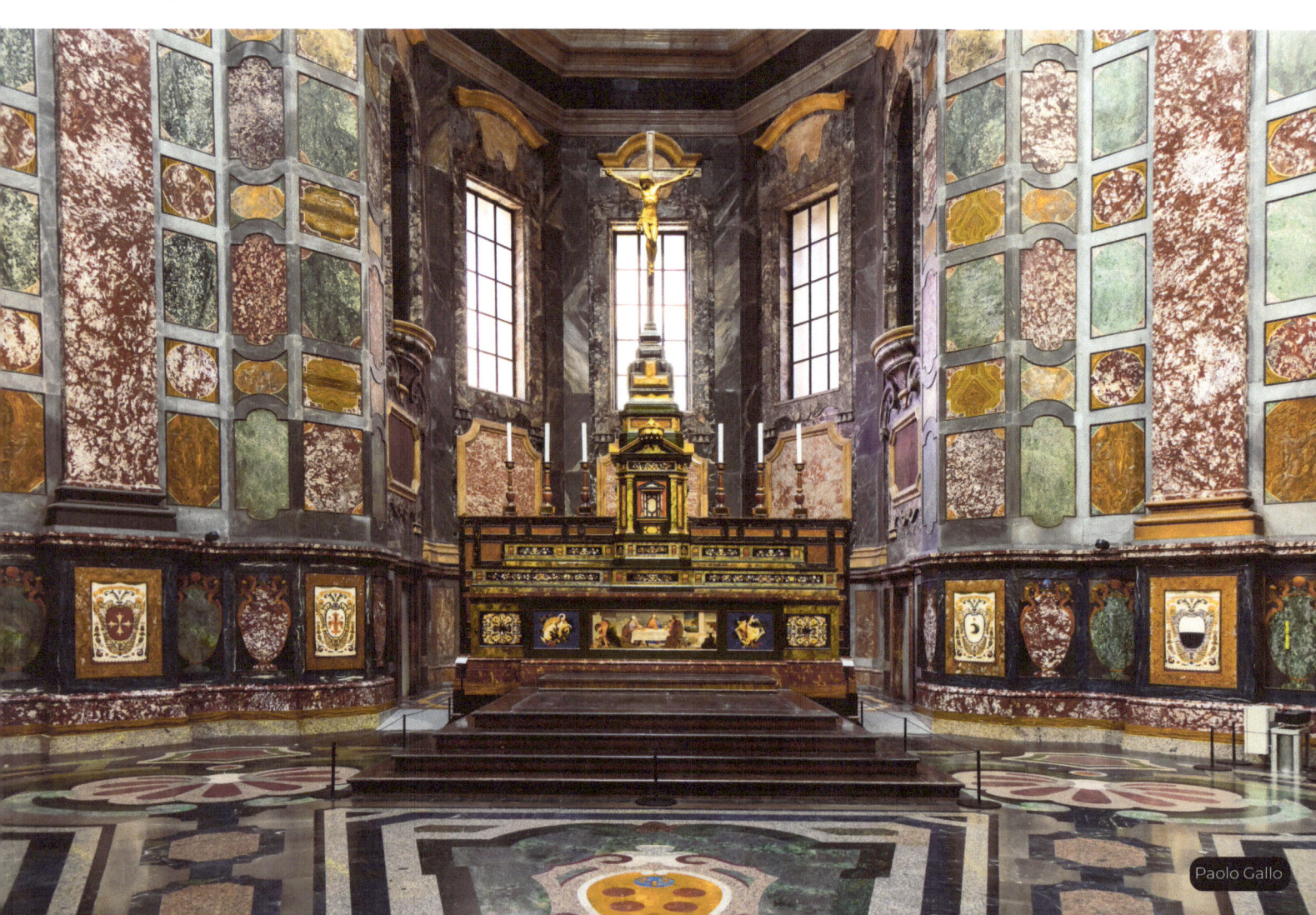

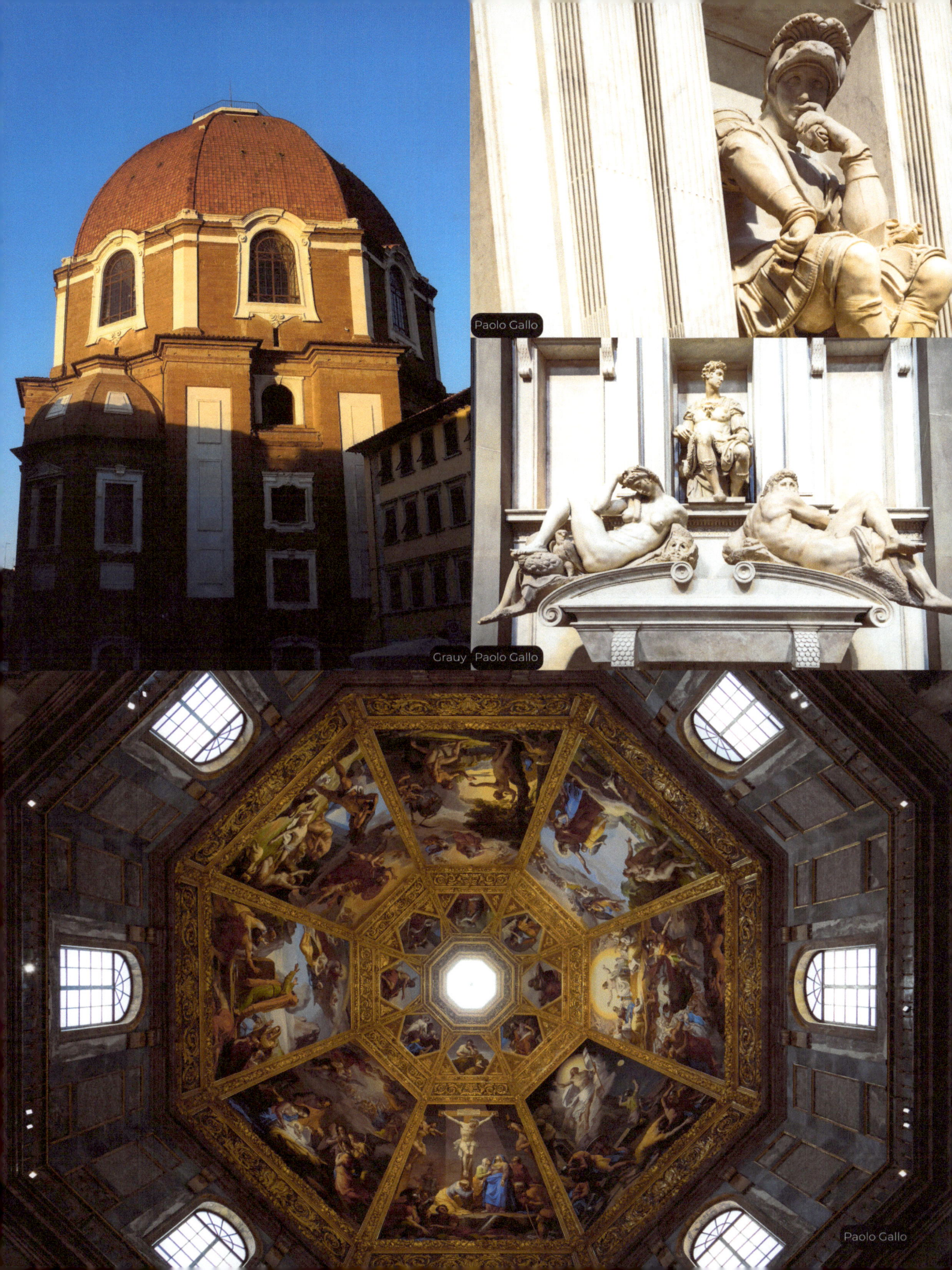

Piazza della Repubblica

In the bustling heart of Florence lies the Piazza della Repubblica, a square rich in history and vibrant with contemporary life. Once the site of the city's ancient Roman forum, it has transformed over the centuries, mirroring the dynamic spirit of Florence itself.

The Piazza della Repubblica is encircled by grand buildings and elegant arcades, remnants of the 19th-century urban renewal that reshaped Florence's medieval core. The triumphal arch, Arcone, stands at one end, inscribed with the words "L'antico centro della città / da secolare squallore / a vita nuova restituito" (The ancient center of the city / restored from age-old squalor / to new life), signifying the area's rejuvenation. This lively square is a melting pot of culture and activity, hosting street performers, artists, and bustling cafes. The historic Café Gilli and Paszkowski offer a glimpse into the artistic past, once frequented by famed writers and intellectuals. The merry-go-round adds a touch of whimsy, enchanting both children and adults alike.

The Piazza della Repubblica is more than a public square; it's a living canvas, capturing the essence of Florentine life. It's a place where history and modernity coalesce, where locals and tourists alike gather to soak in the atmosphere of this ever-evolving city. This square is not just a landmark but the pulsating heart of Florence.

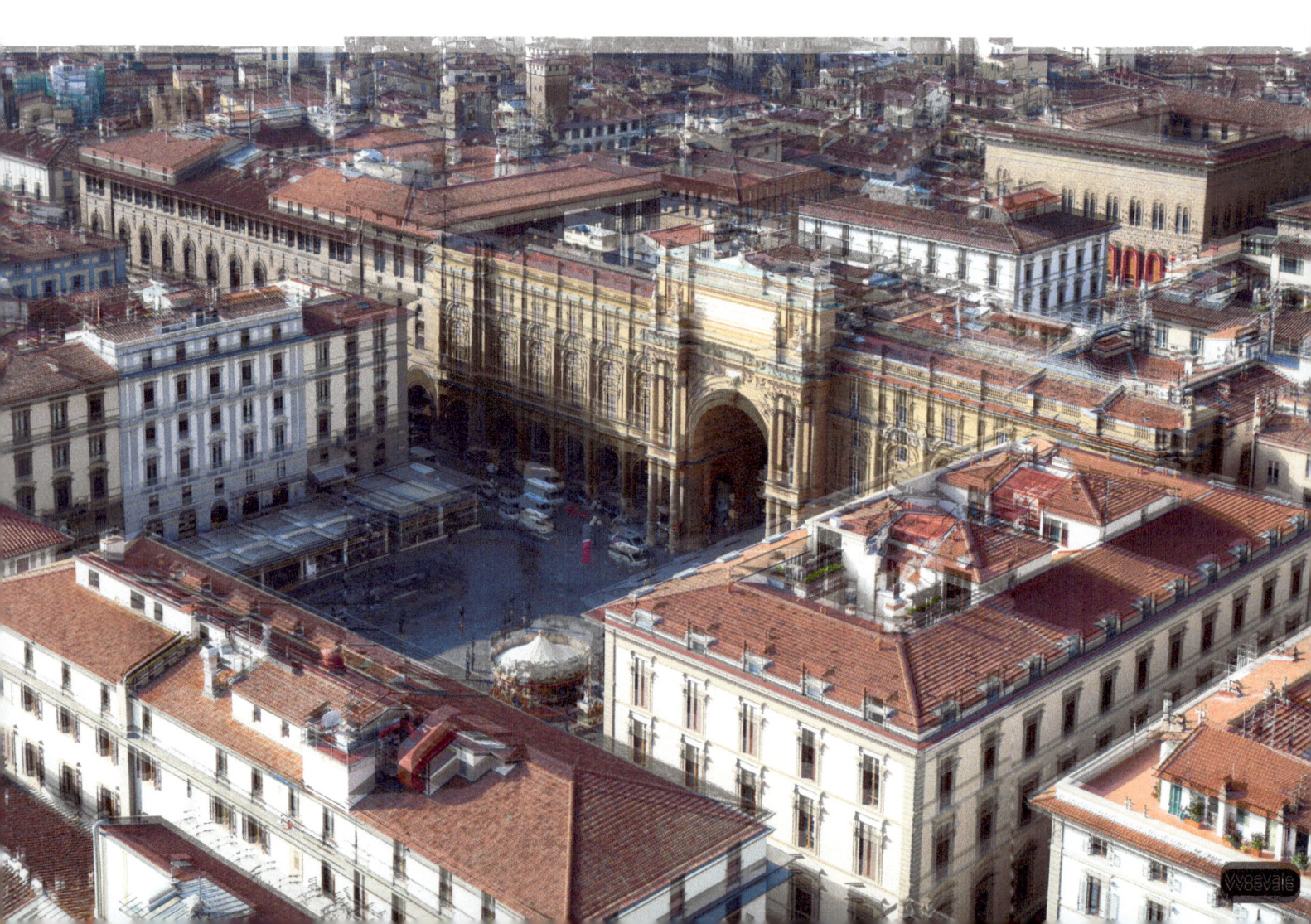

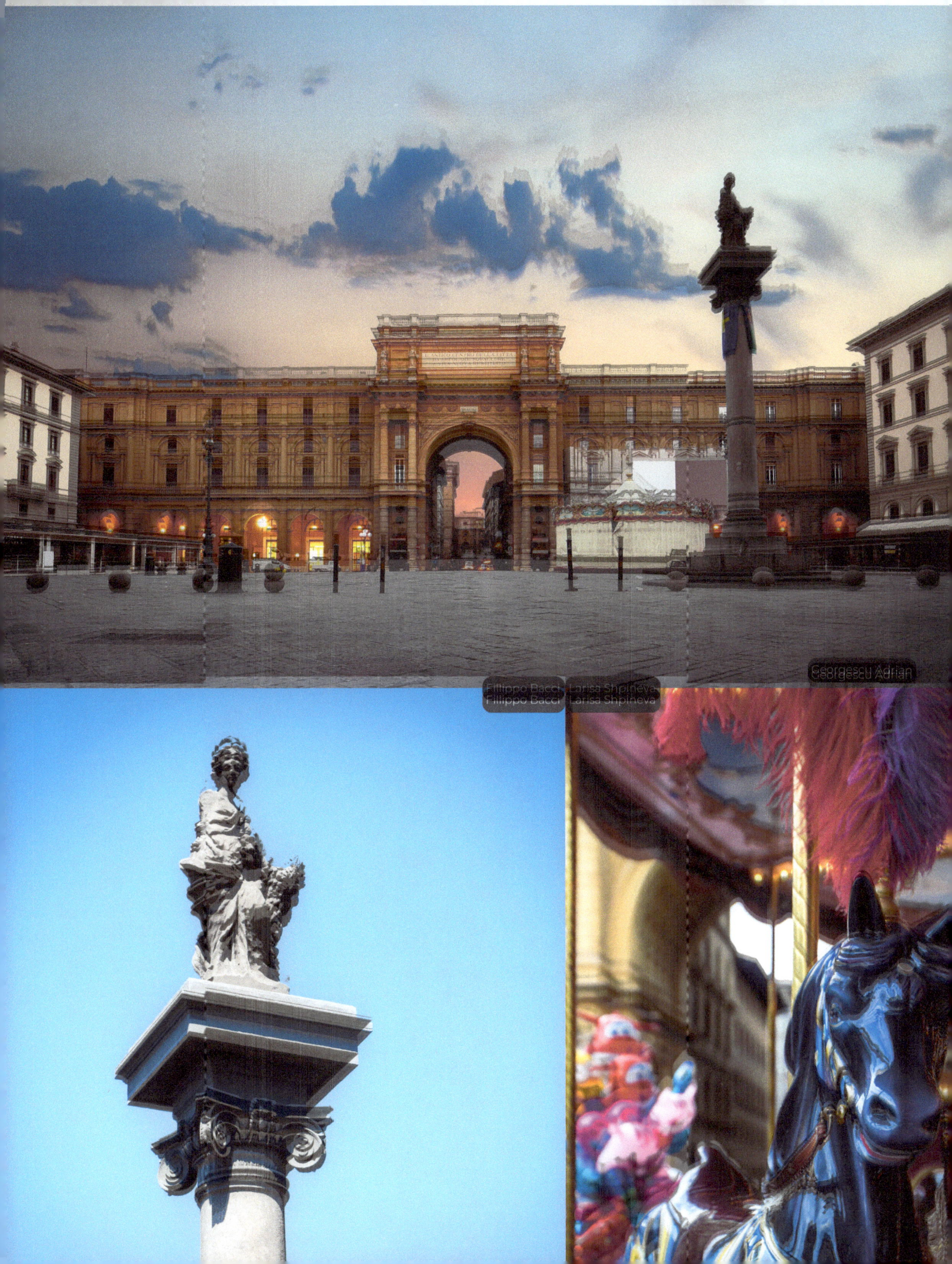

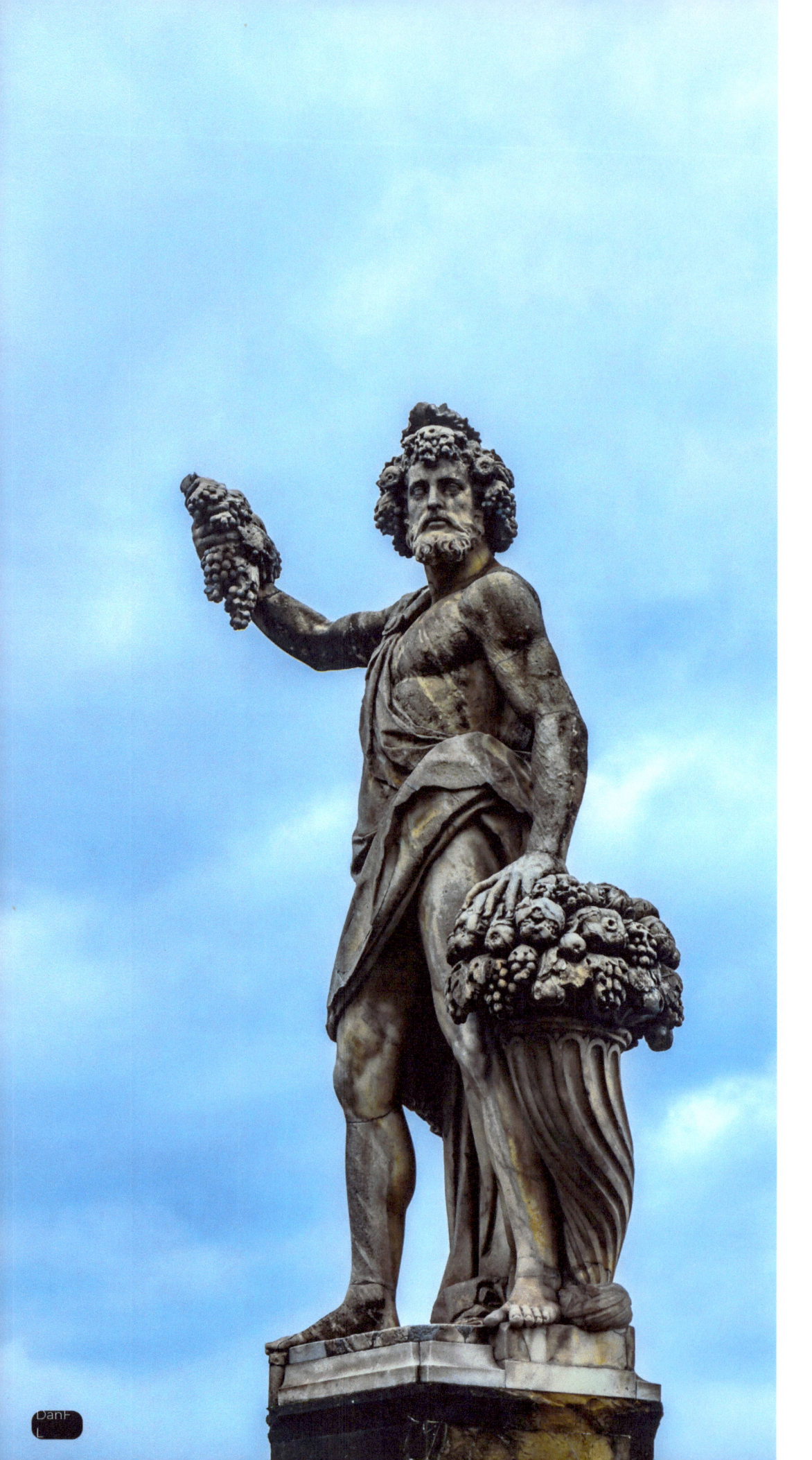

Statue of Bacchus

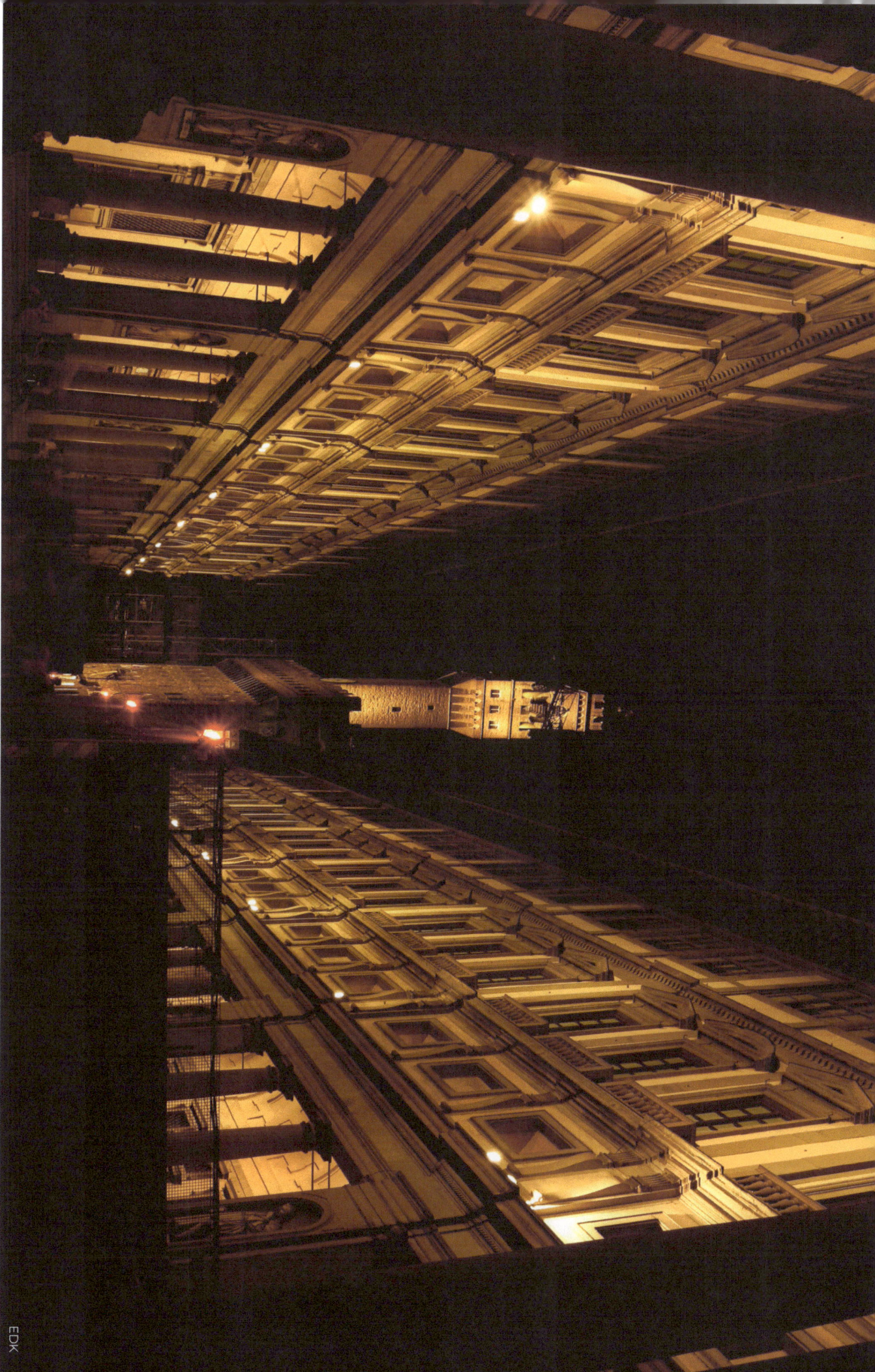

Uffizi Gallery

The Uffizi Gallery, nestled in the heart of Florence, is more than a museum; it's a journey through the Renaissance, a period that reshaped the world of art. Originally designed by Giorgio Vasari in the 16th century as offices for Florentine magistrates, the Uffizi evolved into a gallery housing the art collections of the powerful Medici family, eventually opening to the public in 1769.

As you wander through its hallowed halls, you're walking in the footsteps of history, surrounded by an unparalleled collection of Renaissance masterpieces. The gallery's layout guides visitors through rooms adorned with works by legendary artists such as Giotto, Michelangelo, Leonardo da Vinci, and Raphael.

Notable among its treasures is Botticelli's "The Birth of Venus," a painting that epitomizes Renaissance ideals of beauty and harmony. Each room in the Uffizi offers a new discovery, whether it's Caravaggio's dramatic use of light and shadow or the intricate details in Leonardo's "Annunciation."

The Uffizi isn't just about the past; it's a living dialogue between art and viewer, a testament to the enduring power of human creativity. The gallery's windows also offer scenic views of Florence, a city whose skyline and streetscapes are as much a work of art as the treasures inside. The Uffizi Gallery is a cornerstone of Florence's cultural heritage, a place where art transcends time, igniting imaginations and inspiring generations.

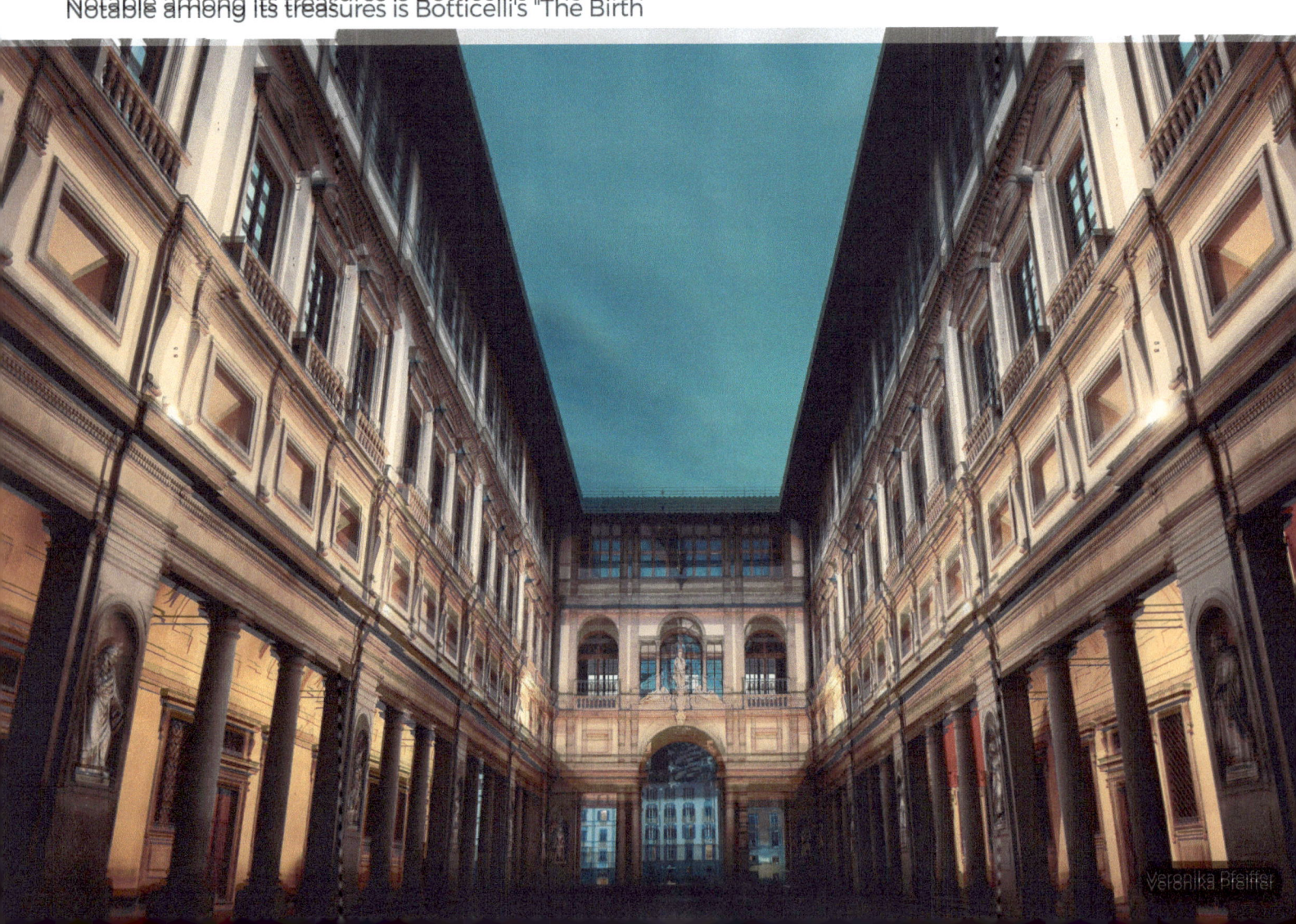

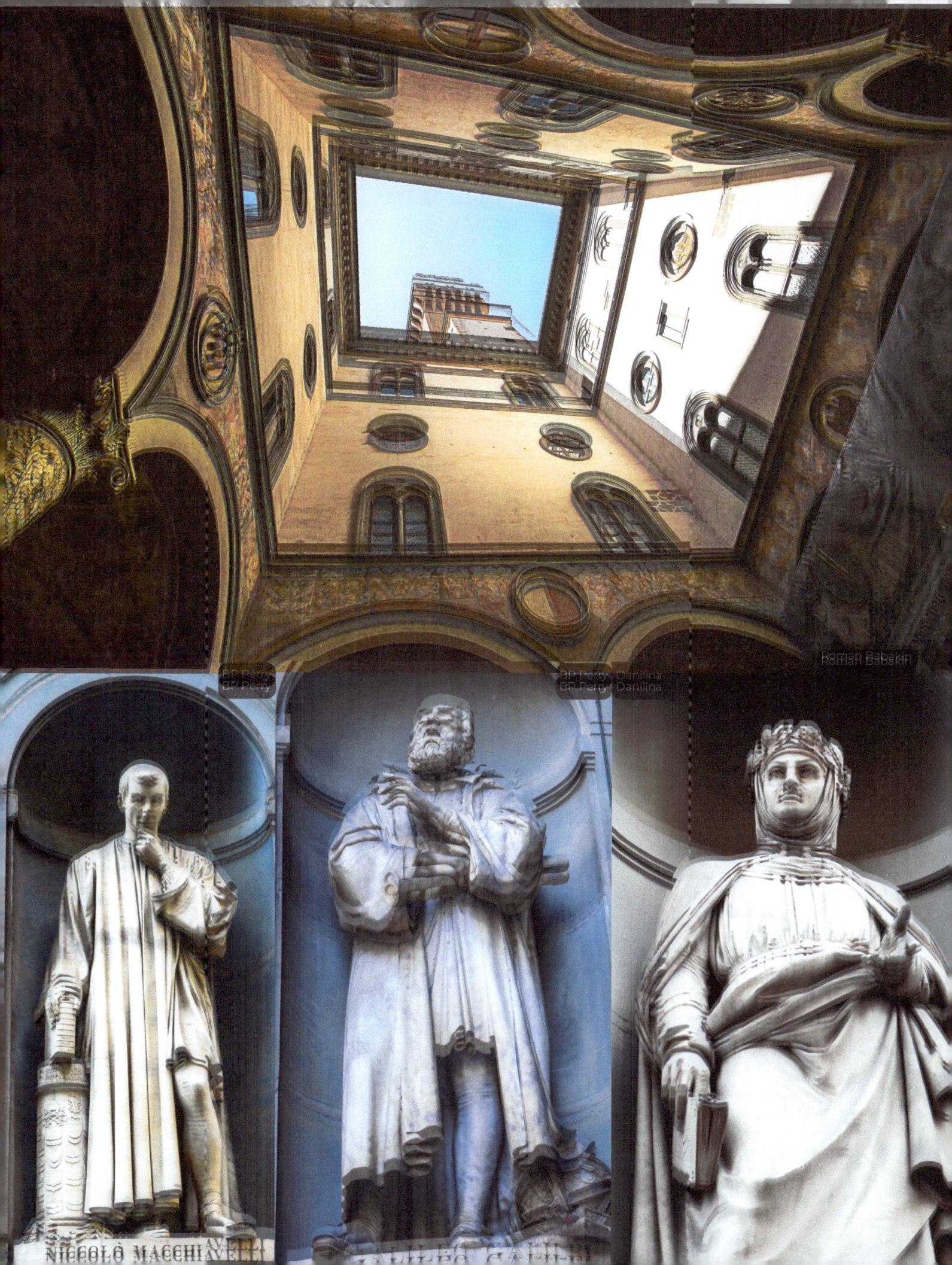

Boboli Gardens

Behind the grand Palazzo Pitti lies the Boboli Gardens, a splendid example of Italian Renaissance landscaping that extends its green embrace over Florence. Created in the 16th century, these gardens are more than a green space; they are an outdoor museum, blending art, nature, and history in a harmonious ensemble.

As you stroll through the Boboli Gardens, every path and hedge seems to tell a story, leading to statues, fountains, and grottoes that surprise and delight. The artistry of the garden's layout showcases the Renaissance ideal of symmetry and order, while offering a serene escape from the city's bustling streets.

Notable features include the Amphitheatre, with an Egyptian obelisk at its heart, and the Neptune Fountain, a testament to the garden's artistic and symbolic ambitions. The Buontalenti Grotto, a fascinating example of Mannerist art, is adorned with stalactites and sculptures, creating an otherworldly experience.

The gardens also offer sweeping views of Florence and the Tuscan hills, a panoramic vista that has inspired artists and poets for centuries. Walking through the Boboli Gardens is like exploring a living canvas, where each turn reveals a new perspective, a fresh burst of beauty, and a deeper connection with Florence's rich artistic heritage.

The Boboli Gardens, with their lush landscapes and artistic treasures, stand as a testament to the ingenuity and vision of the Renaissance, a verdant jewel in the heart of Florence.

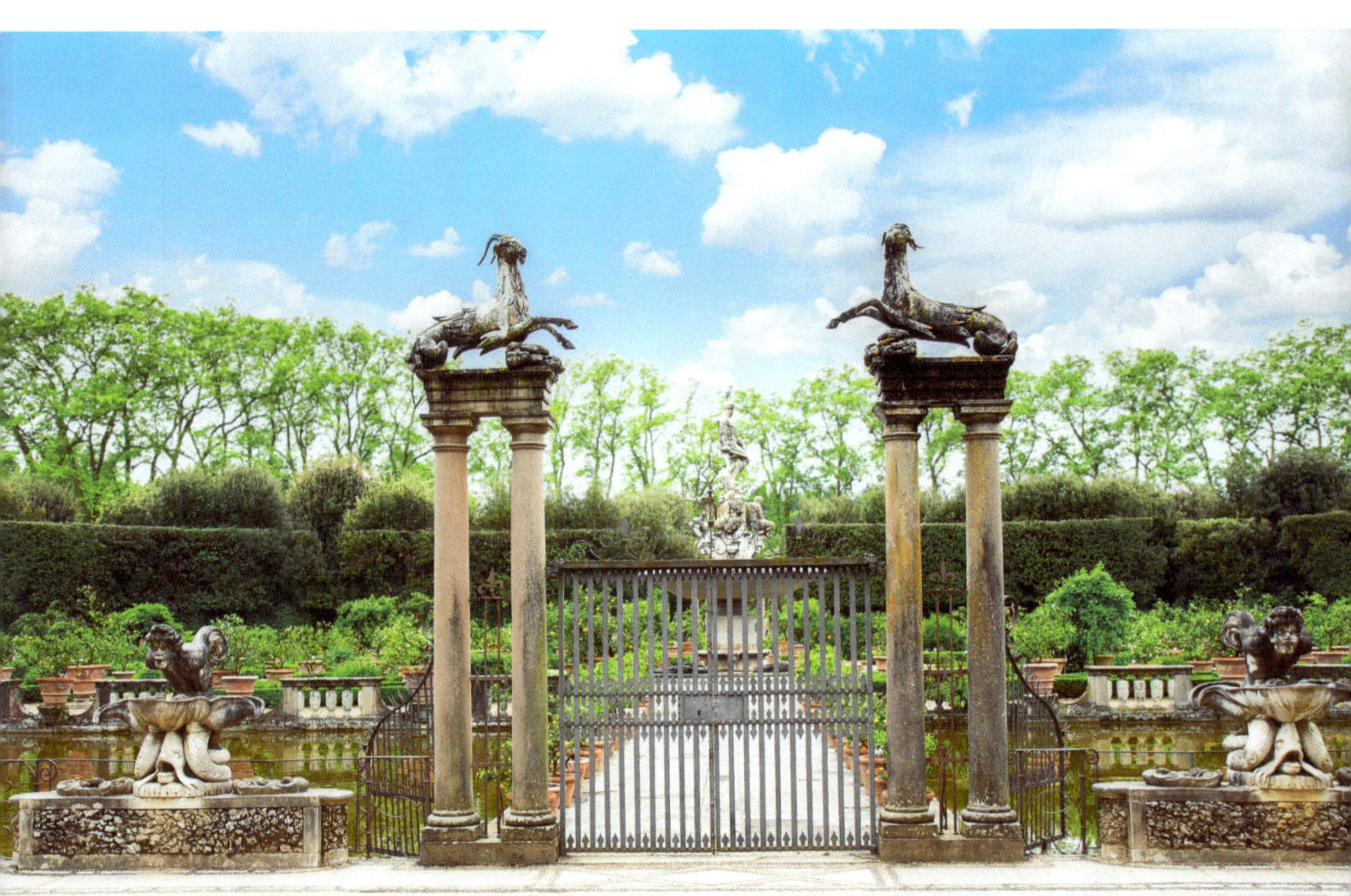

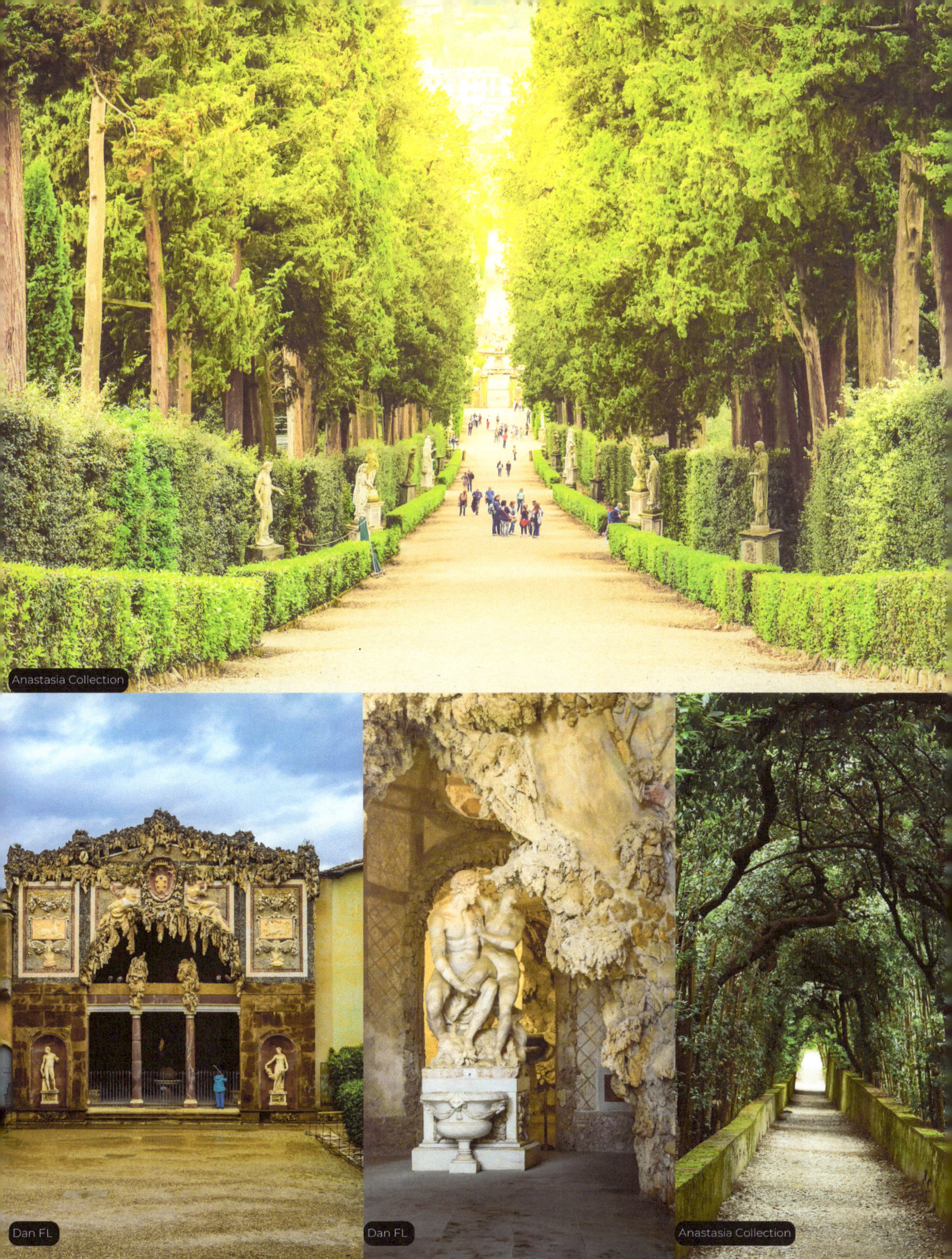

Pitti Palace

Dominating the Oltrarno district of Florence, the Pitti Palace stands as a monumental testament to the city's Renaissance grandeur. Originally built in the mid-15th century for the Pitti family, it was later acquired by the Medici and expanded into a magnificent palace, symbolizing the wealth and power of Florence's ruling class.

This imposing structure, with its rough, stone facade, presents a stark contrast to the ornate interiors, housing an array of museums and galleries. The palace's architecture is a masterful blend of Renaissance design with Baroque and Mannerist elements, reflecting the evolving tastes of its noble inhabitants.

Inside, the Palatine Gallery dazzles with its collection of Renaissance masterpieces, including works by Raphael, Titian, and Rubens, set against the backdrop of sumptuously decorated rooms. The Royal Apartments, still adorned with their original furnishings, offer a glimpse into the life of Florentine nobility.

The palace also serves as the gateway to the Boboli Gardens, a magnificent example of Italianate landscaping. This sprawling green haven, with its fountains, sculptures, and manicured lawns, forms an integral part of the Pitti Palace experience.

The Pitti Palace is not just a building; it's a narrative of power, art, and history, chronicling the rise and fall of Florence's most influential families. Visiting the Pitti Palace is to step into a world of opulence and splendor, a journey through the golden age of the Renaissance.

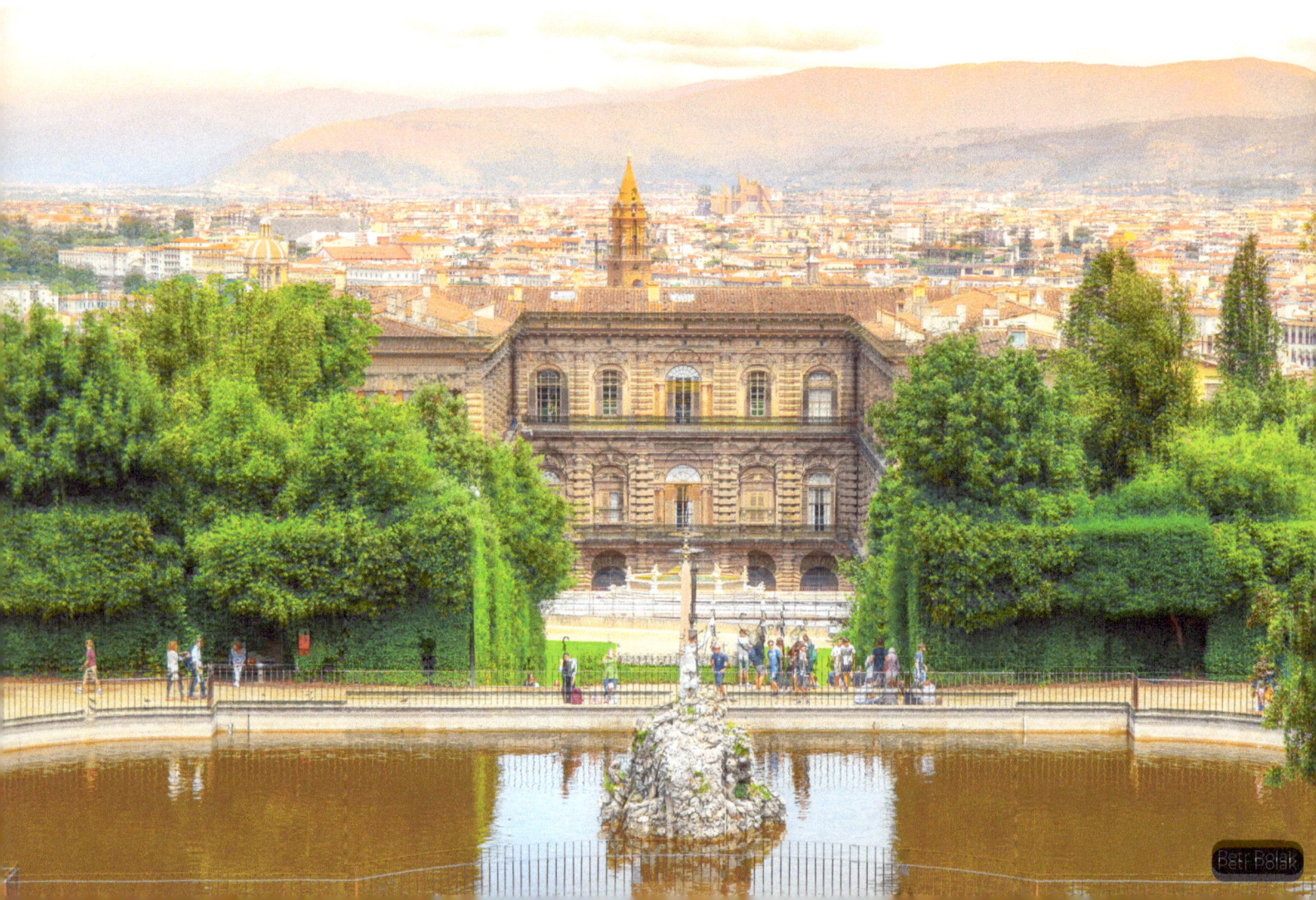

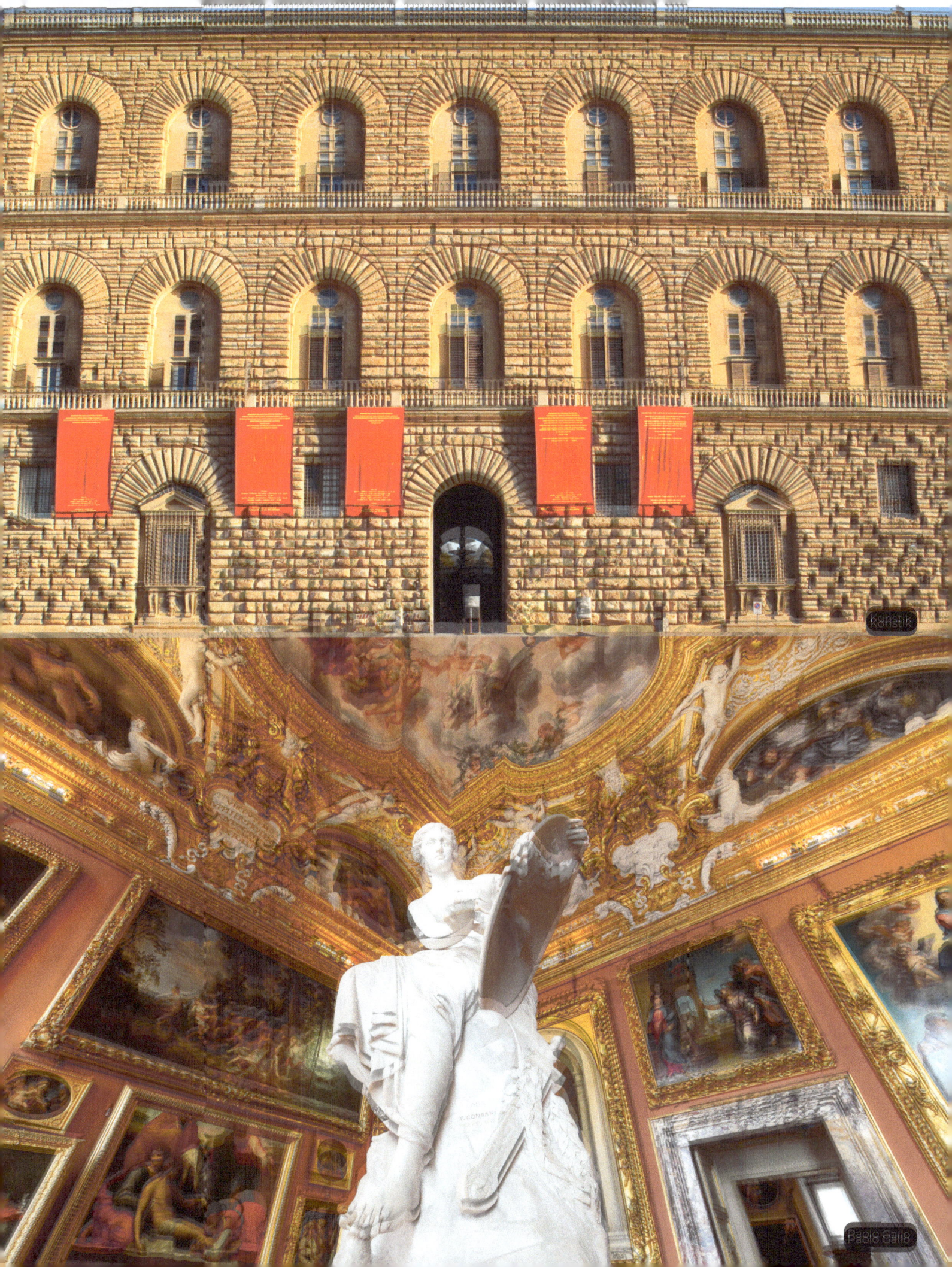

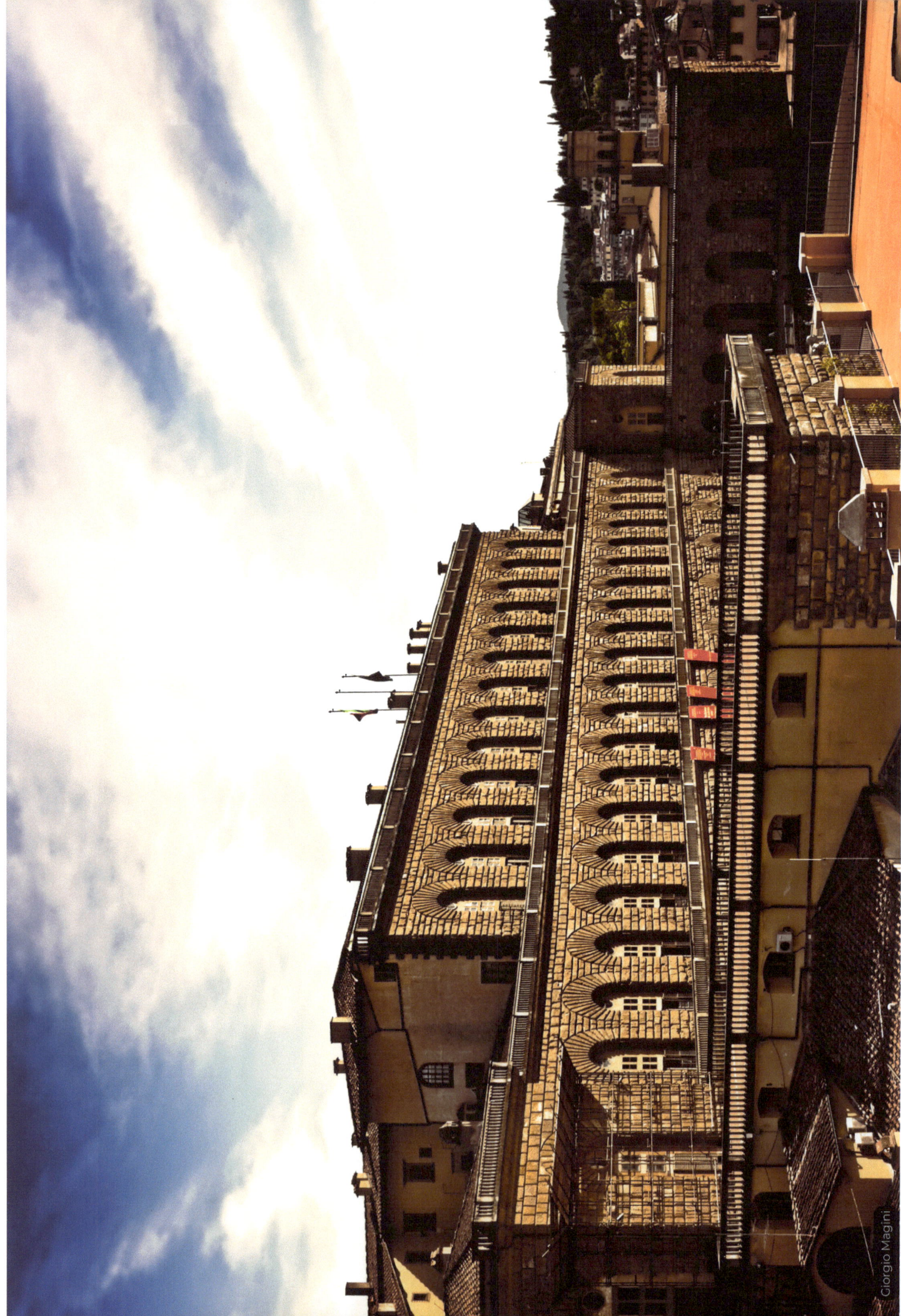

Giorgio Magini

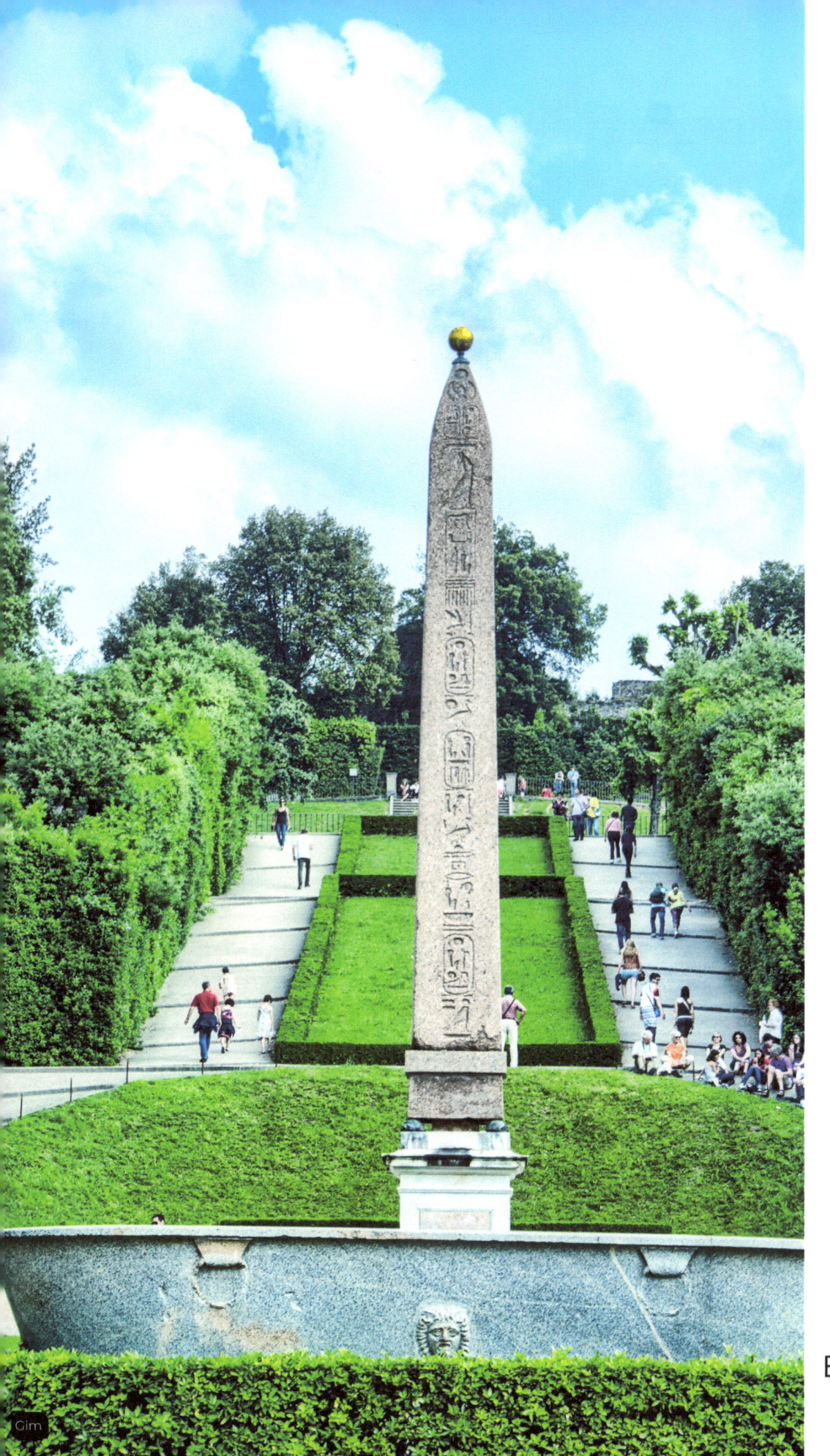

Obelisc in Bobli Gardens Park

Piazza della Signoria

Piazza della Signoria, the heart of Florence's civic life, has stood as the city's political hub since the 14th century. This L-shaped square, framed by historic buildings and adorned with statues, is an open-air gallery showcasing the artistic and political heritage of Florence.

At the center of the square is the majestic Palazzo Vecchio, with its towering Arnolfo Tower, a symbol of the city's enduring power and prestige. This former palace, now a town hall, is flanked by the Loggia dei Lanzi, an outdoor sculpture gallery displaying Renaissance masterpieces, including Cellini's "Perseus with the Head of Medusa" and Giambologna's "Rape of the Sabine Women."

The square is also home to a replica of Michelangelo's David, standing at the entrance of the Palazzo Vecchio, a powerful reminder of the original's significance as a symbol of the Republic's defiance against larger foes.

Piazza della Signoria has been a witness to key historical events, including the Bonfire of the Vanities and the dramatic fall of the Medici. Today, it remains a lively space, bustling with cafes, street performers, and throngs of tourists, drawn to its rich history and artistic legacy.

A visit to Piazza della Signoria is an immersive experience into the heart of Florence, where art, history, and daily life intertwine, offering a unique glimpse into the soul of this Renaissance city.

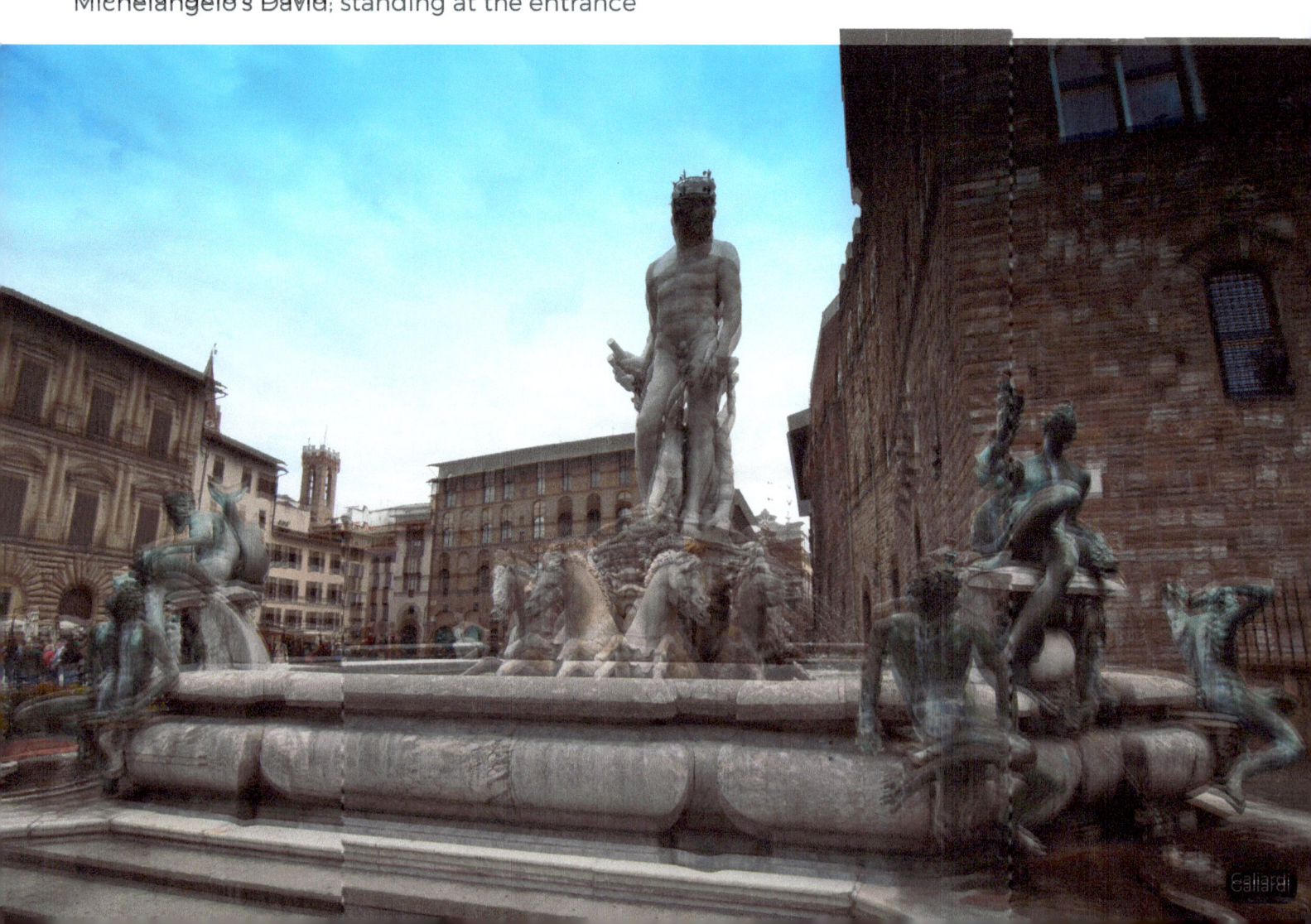

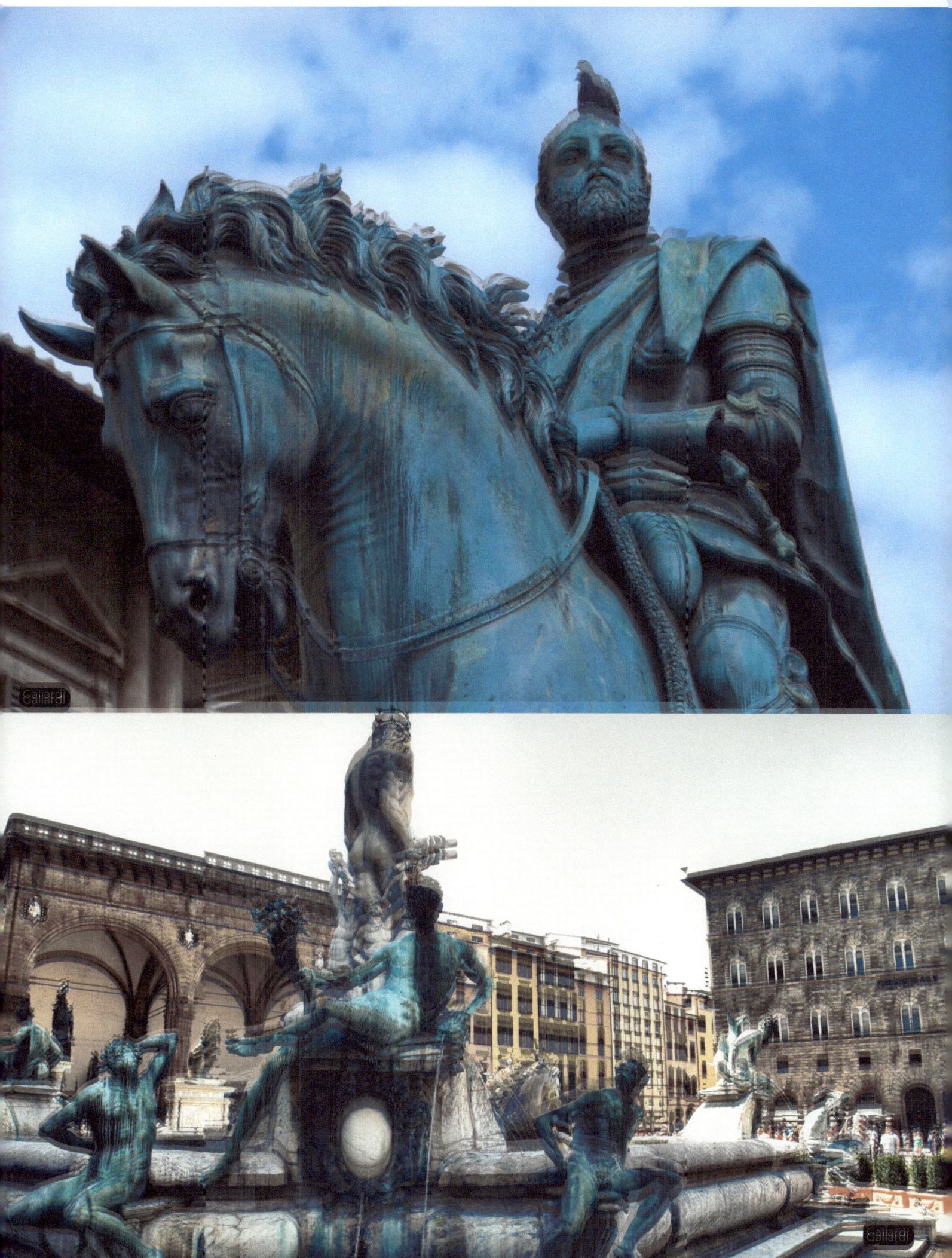

Santa Maria Novella Church

Santa Maria Novella, located just across from Florence's main railway station, stands as a magnificent representation of Gothic elegance blended with Renaissance artistry. Founded by the Dominican Order in the 13th century, this church is a treasure trove of artistic and architectural wonders.

The church's facade, a masterful creation by Leon Battista Alberti, is a harmonious blend of white and green marble, presenting a perfect example of early Renaissance architectural principles. Alberti's design, with its classical symmetry and proportion, complements the Gothic structure, creating a visually stunning entrance.

Inside, Santa Maria Novella is a sanctuary of art. It houses Masaccio's "Trinity," a groundbreaking fresco known for its early use of linear perspective, a technique that revolutionized Renaissance painting. The Tornabuoni Chapel, adorned with frescoes by Ghirlandaio, tells biblical stories with a Florentine twist, featuring contemporary landscapes and local notables.

Each chapel and altar within the church is a testament to the artistic ferment of the time, displaying works by Giotto, Brunelleschi, and Filippino Lippi. The church's cloisters, including the serene Green Cloister and the frescoed Spanish Chapel, offer a quiet retreat, rich in artistic and historical significance.

Santa Maria Novella is not just a church; it's a gallery of medieval and Renaissance art, a place where every corner reveals a story, every fresco a glimpse into the past. This church embodies the spirit of Florence, a city where faith and art are eternally intertwined.

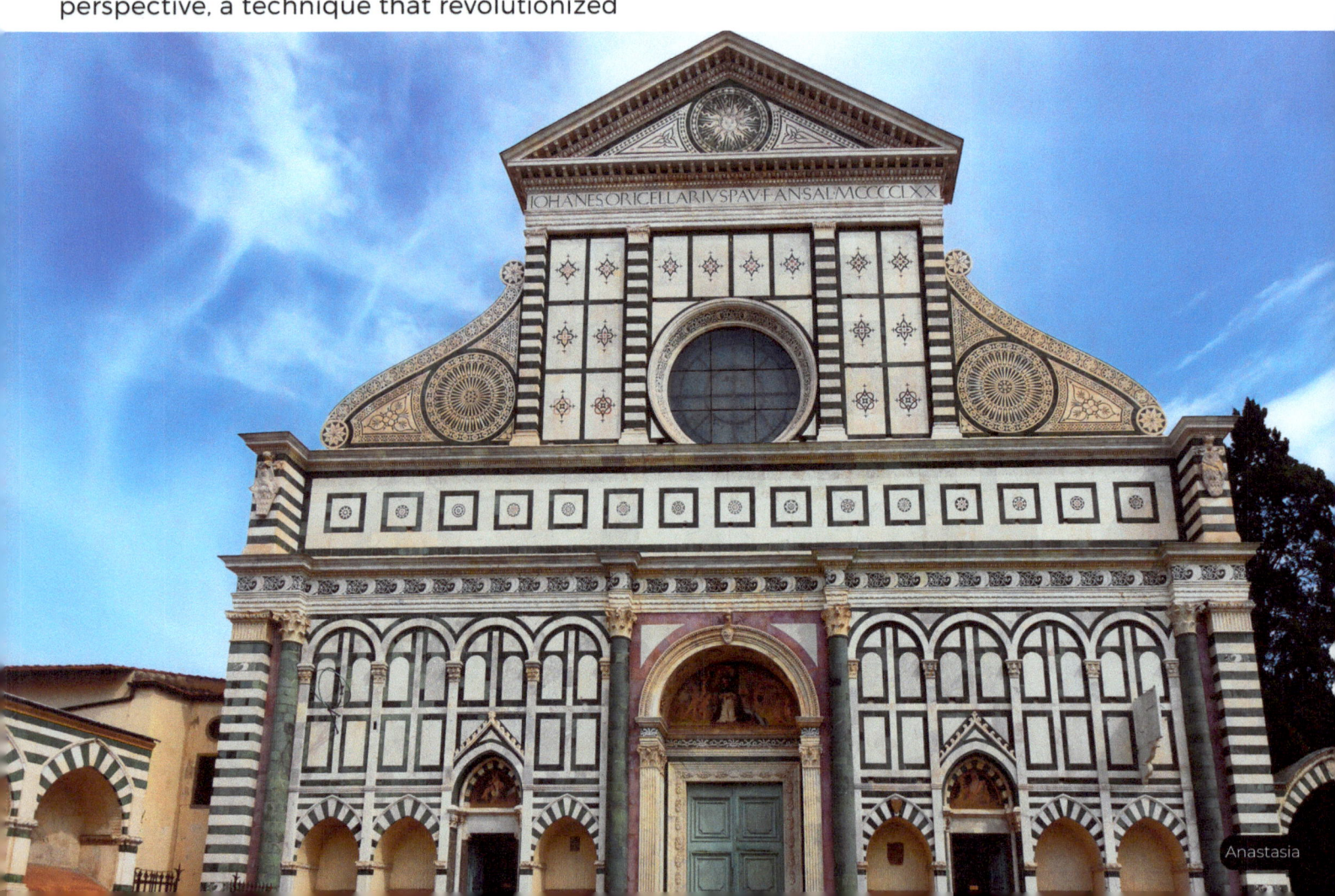

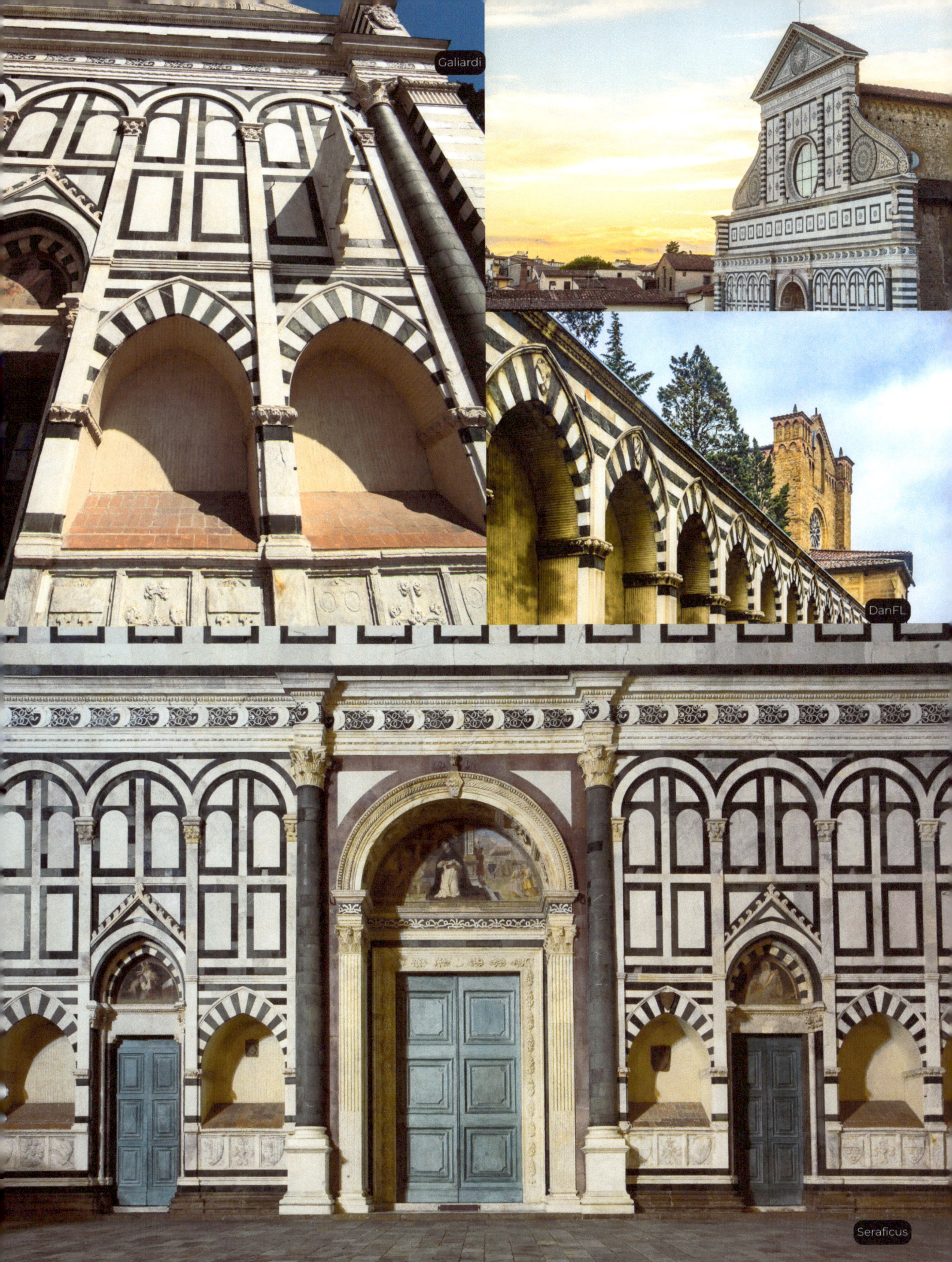

Basilica of Santa Croce

The Basilica of Santa Croce, nestled in the heart of Florence, is not only a principal place of worship but also a mausoleum of Italy's most illustrious figures. This 14th-century Franciscan church, renowned for its Florentine Gothic style, is an emblem of the city's rich historical and cultural tapestry.

The church's façade, a striking pattern of red, green, and white marble, is a later addition that splendidly encapsulates the spirit of the Renaissance. Inside, the vast nave opens up to an array of chapels, each a testament to the artistic prowess of the times. The walls and ceilings are adorned with frescoes by Giotto and his pupils, depicting scenes of serenity and devotion.

Santa Croce is also known as the Temple of the Italian Glories, the final resting place of luminaries such as Michelangelo, Galileo, Machiavelli, and Rossini. Their tombs are not just burial sites but artworks themselves, celebrating the lives and contributions of these great individuals.

The Pazzi Chapel, designed by Brunelleschi, stands as a masterpiece of Renaissance architecture, with its harmonious proportions and use of space. The cloisters and the Last Supper Museum further add to the basilica's allure, inviting visitors to explore and reflect.

Visiting the Basilica of Santa Croce is a journey through Italian history, art, and spirituality. Each tomb, painting, and sculpture tells a story, contributing to the narrative of Florence as a cradle of culture and intellect.

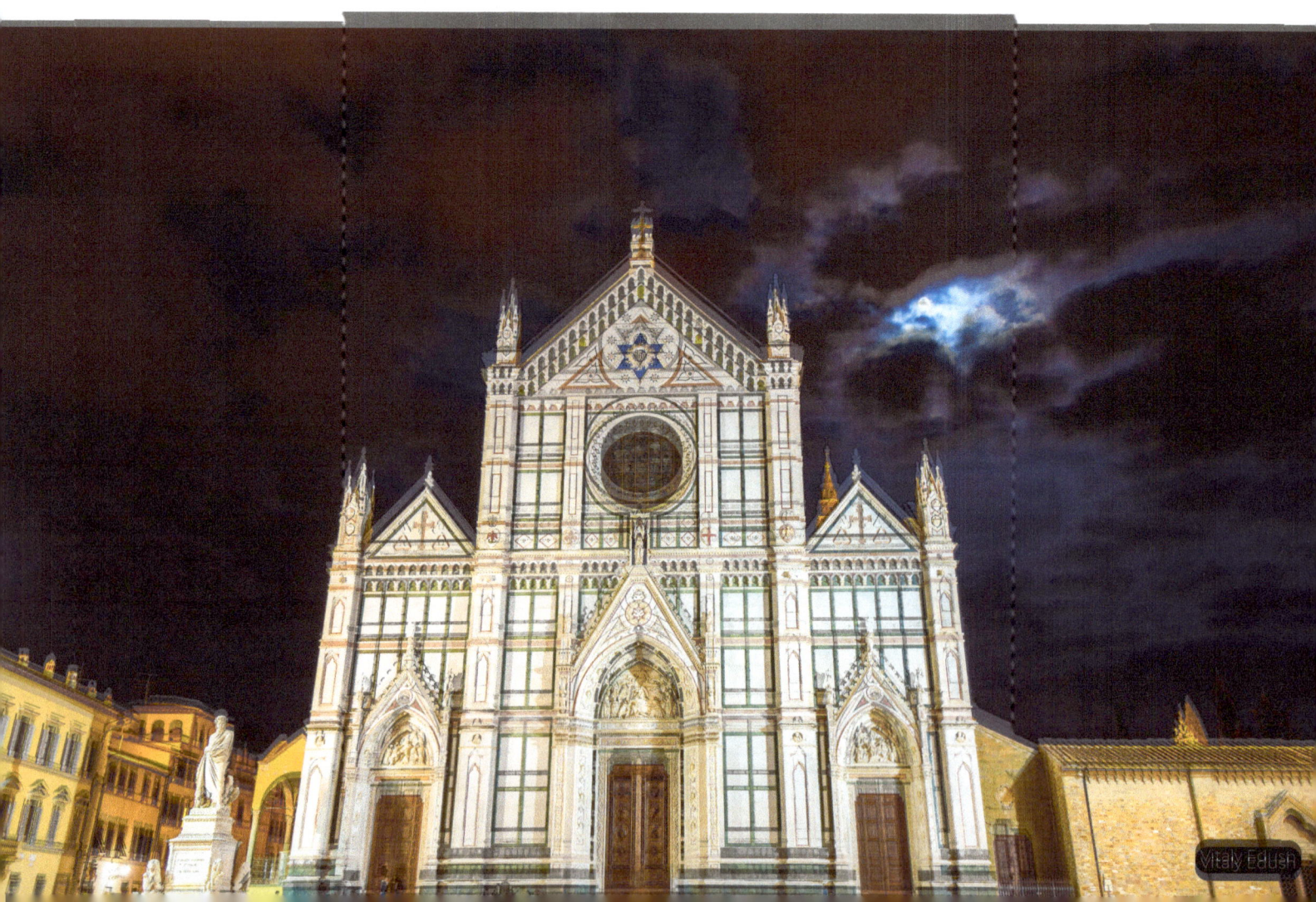

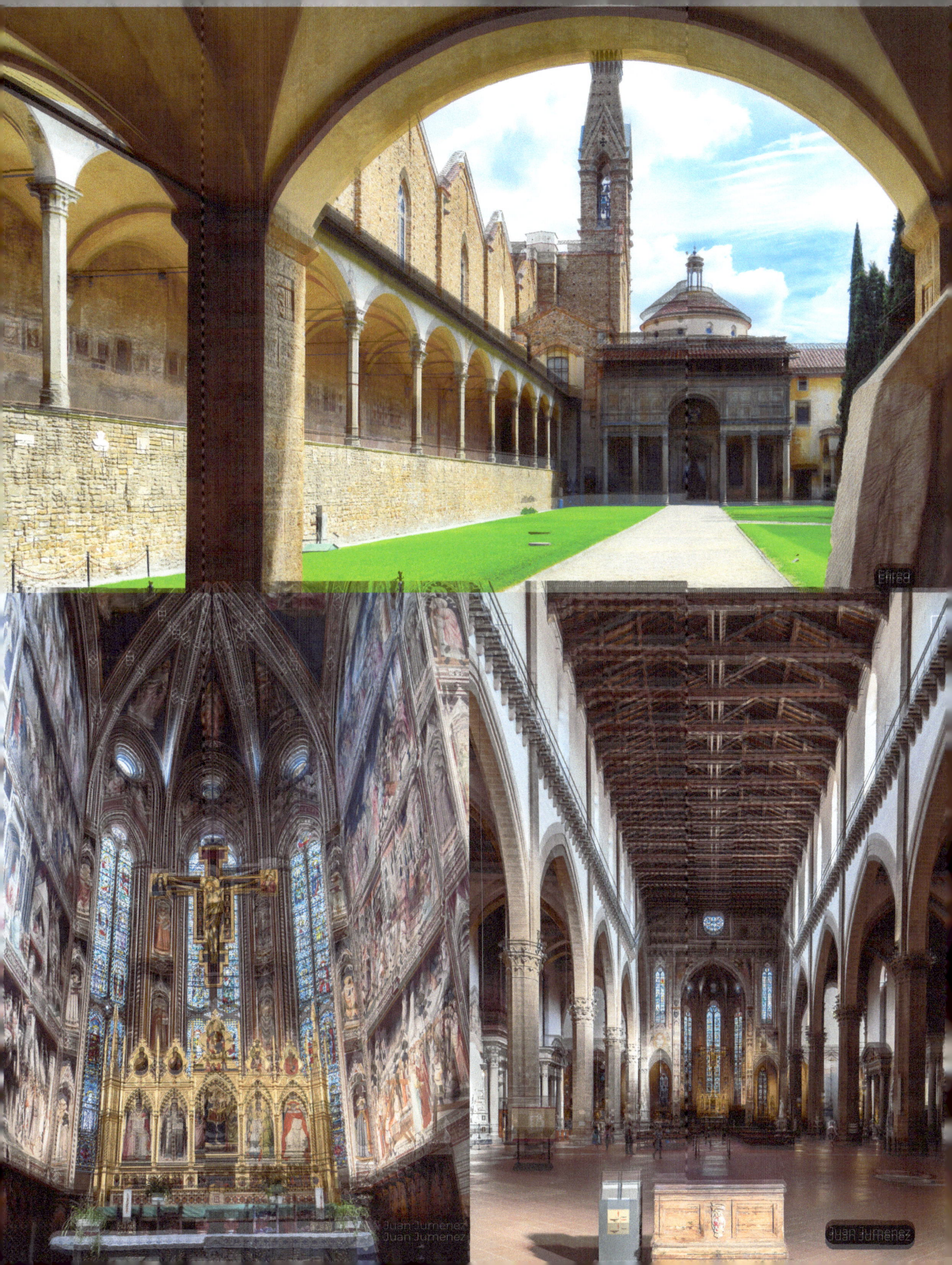

"Discovering Florence - The Cradle of The Renaissance Pictorial" has offered a visual and narrative journey through Florence's timeless splendor, from the majestic Duomo to the tranquil Boboli Gardens. For those yearning to delve deeper into the heart of this Renaissance gem, "UNVEILING FLORENCE - Your Travel Guide to The Cradle of The Renaissance" is your essential companion. This guide unlocks hidden alleys, unveils lesser-known stories, and reveals new facets of famous attractions, enriching your exploration of Florence. Let "UNVEILING FLORENCE" be your key to discovering new beauty and experiencing the city's enchanting allure in ways you never imagined. Your journey into the Renaissance soul of Florence continues here.

UNVEILING FLORENCE
Your Travel Guide to The Cradle of The Renaissance

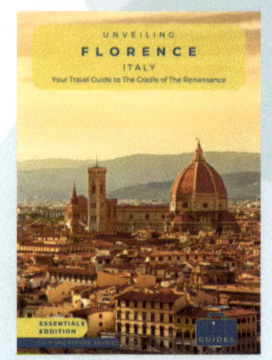

CHECK OUT THE FRANCE UNVEILED TRAVEL GUIDES SERIES

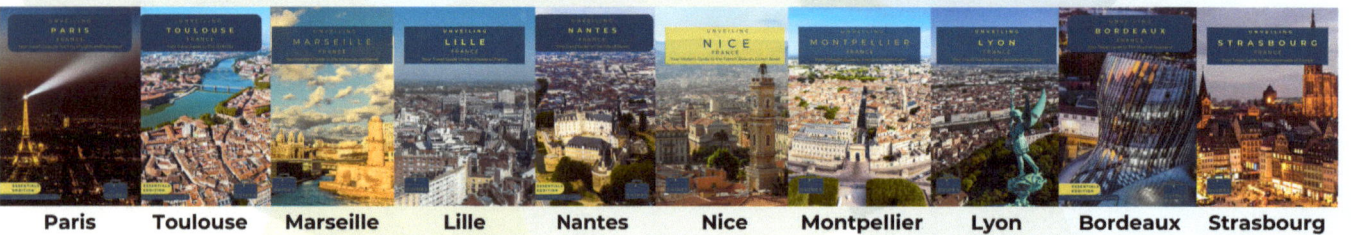

Paris · Toulouse · Marseille · Lille · Nantes · Nice · Montpellier · Lyon · Bordeaux · Strasbourg

CHECK OUT THE ITALY UNCOVERED TRAVEL GUIDES SERIES

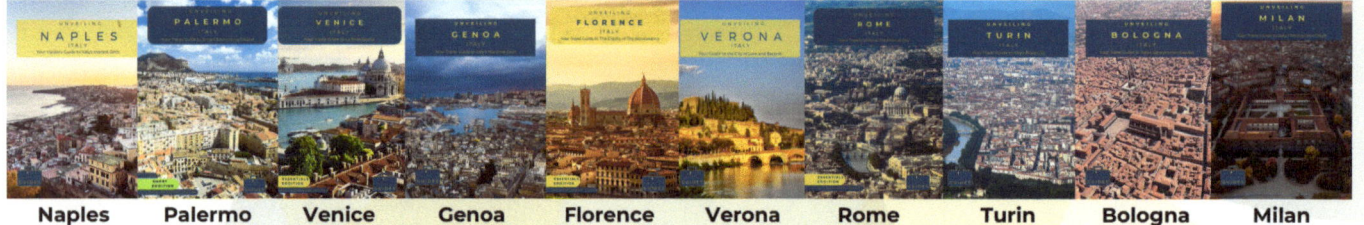

Naples · Palermo · Venice · Genoa · Florence · Verona · Rome · Turin · Bologna · Milan

CHECK OUT THE SPAIN UNVEILED TRAVEL GUIDES SERIES

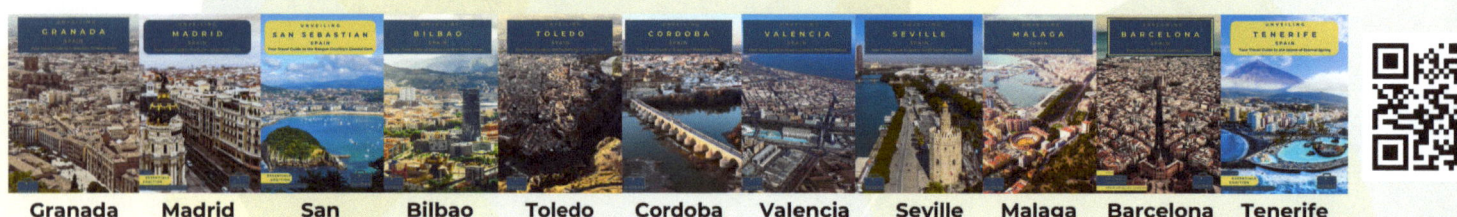

Granada · Madrid · San Sebastian · Bilbao · Toledo · Cordoba · Valencia · Seville · Malaga · Barcelona · Tenerife

Join our Tailored Travel Guides Network for more benefits by accessing this link:
https://mailchi.mp/d151cba349e8/ttgnetwork
Or by scanning the QR code

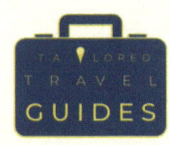

Discover your journey!

www.ingramcontent.com/pod-product-compliance
Lightning Source LLC
Chambersburg PA
CBHW051932210526
45473CB00006B/2228